# KIERAN BEVILLE

# DEVELOPING HEALTHY CHURCHES

## A Case-Study in Revelation

# DEVELOPING HEALTHY CHURCHES

## A Case Study in Revelation

**Kieran Beville**

Christian Publishing House

Cambridge, Ohio

*Christian Publishing House*

Professional Christian Publishing of the Good News

*DEVELOPING HEALTHY CHURCHES A Case Study in Revelation*

Publishing by Christian Publishing House

ISBN-13: 978-0692342985

ISBN-10: 0692342982

## Dedication

I dedicate this work to my students at Tyndale Theological Seminary, Badhoevedorp, Netherlands. I hope it will assist in developing healthy churches.

# Table of Content

# Endorsements

Kieran Beville is rightly concerned that the main source for a definition of and a strategy for a healthy church should be Scripture itself and that is what lies behind these deceptively simple expositions of the letters to the churches of Revelation. They are eminently accessible and readable but get you deep into the text and the background from which they came. As he opens up this section of Revelation, he does what all good preaching should do – he teaches the mind, touches the heart and targets the will. Kieran Beville helpfully reviews and assesses the current trends in the church health movement, but worth the price of the book alone is the chapter on finding an Interpretative Approach to Revelation, which is the best summary and critique of the various schools of interpretation of the many that I have read.—**John Brand, Principal, Edinburgh Bible College**

Kieran Beville's study of the letters to the 7 churches in Revelation 2 and 3 is full of practical instruction that flows out of his exposition of this fascinating portion of scripture. Beginning with a very helpful discussion of "the church health movement," he then proceeds with an overview of the major interpretive positions found among evangelicals regarding the book of Revelation, argues for the futurist position and proceeds accordingly, concluding with a concise exposition of what is a healthy church. His writing throughout is clear and his explanations are easy to follow. He excels at applying the contents of these ancient letters to real life situations in today's church. This is a helpful study and worthwhile reading for anyone who wants to know what the risen Lord requires of his people at this point in redemptive history."

**Rev. Dr Kirk Wellum, Principal, Toronto Baptist Seminary and Bible College.**

# Foreword

My personal view is that the main purpose of a book's Foreword should be to explain why any reader should invest his/her time and energy reading the pages that follow. With respect to *Developing Healthy Churches: A Case Study in Revelation* I find two compelling reasons. The first is theological, the second, application.

In his book, author Kieran Beville establishes a solid theological foundation for Christian application of his teachings. In laying a foundation for what follows, Beville succinctly and clearly presents the arguments supporting the four major competing perspectives or "interpretive models" of Revelation. They include the idealist, preterist, historicist and futurist perspectives. After presenting the evidence for and against each of the perspectives, he explains why he opts for the futurist perspective or model. In that decision, I believe he is correct and wins the debate with proponents of the other perspectives by showing how they are inconsistent with the clearly stated implications of 2 Timothy 3:16.

Having effectively justified his Revelation theology, Beville focuses on lessons Christians should be learning from the history of the seven churches of Asia Minor. In his straightforward exegesis and exposition of Revelation chapters 2 and 3, he makes numerous inferences that help describe the spiritual condition of the church from the perspective of its Head and Master, the living Jesus Christ.

Irrespective of the reader's role or position in the Church, I believe *Developing Healthy Churches* will contribute to a more mature understanding of God's Word in general and the Book of Revelation in particular.

**Dr Gene A. Getz**

# Origins and Development of the Church Health Movement

Where has the "church health" movement come from and where is it going to? Influential writers on this subject, such as Gene Getz, John McArthur, Mark Dever and others all seem to have different understandings of what, exactly, constitutes a healthy church.[1] Theological perspective and practical pastoral experience will shape one's understanding of church health. There may be some overlap with regard to core elements among some writers but no two lists of healthy characteristics will look exactly the same.[2]

Many people, in a variety of disciplines, have tried to define health. One dictionary definition is, "physical and mental well-being, freedom from disease, and normality of physical and mental functions."[3] A thesaurus lists, "...vigor, wholeness, fitness, robustness, stamina, and wellness."[4] In

---

[1] Some early books on church health include the following: Barry Campbell, *Smaller Churches Healthy and Growing* (Nashville, TN: LifeWay Press, 1998); Gerald Neal Hewitt, *A Prescription for Healthy Churches: Help for Disintegrating Churches and Directionless Pastors* (Winston-Salem, NC: GNH Publishing, 2001); and Peter Masters, *Do We Have a Policy for Church Health & Growth: Paul's Ten Point Policy* (London: The Wakeman Trust, 2002).

[2] Indeed my selection comes from my theological perspective and practical pastoral experience.

[3] David B. Guralnik, ed., *Webster's New World Dictionary*, 2d college ed. (New York, NY: Simon and Schuster, 1984), 644.

[4] Carlton Laird, ed., *Webster's New World Thesaurus*, rev. ed., updated by William D. Lutz (New York, NY: Simon & Schuster, 1971), 346.

1974 the World Health Organization defined health as, "...a state of complete physical, mental, and social well-being and not merely the absence of disease."

While definitions of physical health may prove useful in defining church health, the main source of a definition must be the Bible. Non-biblical principles can add important ideas, but the foundation of the definition must be Scripture itself.

In *The Purpose Driven Church*, Rick Warren said that "the key issue for churches in the twenty-first century will be church health, not church growth."[5] Warren believed that focusing on church growth alone was wrong. He added, "When congregations are healthy, they grow the way God intends....If your church is genuinely healthy, you won't have to worry about it growing."[6]

In 1972, Ray Stedman briefly discussed the subject of church health in his book, *Body Life*.[7] In his chapter entitled "Keeping the Body Healthy," Stedman wrote:

> No athlete spends all his time running races or playing the game for which he is trained; he must also spend many hours keeping himself in shape and developing his skills to a high degree. So it is with the body of Christ. The work of the ministry will never be properly done by a weak and unhealthy church,

---

[5] Rick Warren, *The Purpose Driven Church: Growth without Compromising Your Message & Mission* (Grand Rapids, MI: Zondervan Publishing House, 1995), 17.

[6] Ibid.

[7] Ray C. Stedman, "Keeping the Body Healthy," In *Body Life: The Church Comes Alive!* (Ventura, CA: Regal Books, 1972).

torn with internal pains, and wracked by spiritual diseases.[8]

At the conclusion Stedman added, "A healthy body is necessary to do effective work."[9]

In 1973 Donald McGavran and Win Arn addressed the subject of church health in their book *How to Grow a Church: Conversations about Church Growth.*[10]

Three years later C. Peter Wagner proposed seven vital signs as a gauge of a healthy church in his book, *Your Church Can Grow: Seven Vital Signs of a Healthy Church.*[11] However, while Wagner mentioned church health in his book, his primarily emphasis was church growth not church health.

Over the next two decades, numerous books and articles continued to be written on church growth. Church health became a forgotten subject. A renewed emphasis on church health began with the publication of books by Dan Spader and Gary Mayes (1991) and Leith Anderson (1992).[12] Soon other books dealing with church health were published by Rick Warren (1995), Christian Schwarz (1996); Mark Dever (1998) and Steven Macchia (1999)[13] Since then numerous

---

[8] Ibid., 106.

[9] Ibid., 114.

[10] Donald A. McGavran and Win Arn, *How to Grow a Church: Conversations about Church Growth* (Glendale, CA: Regal Books, 1973).

[11] C. Peter Wagner, *Your Church Can Grow: Seven Vital Signs of a Healthy Church* (Glendale, CA: Regal Books, 1976).

[12] Dan Spader and Gary Mayes, *Growing a Healthy Church* (Chicago: Moody Press, 1991) and Leith Anderson, "Is This Body Healthy?" chap. in *A Church for the 21st Century* (Minneapolis, MN: Bethany House Publishers, 1992).

[13] Rick Warren, *The Purpose Driven Church*; Christian A. Schwarz, *Natural Church Development: A Guide to Eight Essential Qualities of Healthy Churches* (Carol Stream, IL: ChurchSmart Resources, 1996); Mark

authors have written about church health. However, these writers have kudos because their works were/are seminal

However, in spite of the availability of many books on the subject, there is no universally agreed, comprehensive definition of church health. There are a diverse range of definitions and criteria for evaluating church health but no dominant consensus. It is surprising that many works about church health omit any treatment of the Words of Jesus to the seven churches in Asia Minor. These chapters in the book of Revelation speak directly to the very core of the matter and are critical to a proper understanding of what constitutes a healthy church. Furthermore, a lack of rigorous research has created principles of questionable value and conflicting ideas. The current confusion over the definition of a healthy church hinders the effectiveness of the movement. Conservative, traditional, attraction churches have their understanding of what constitutes a healthy church and anything that deviates from that is viewed with suspicion. New expressions of church, such as seeker-centered (perhaps not so "new" now), emerging and missional gatherings reject conservative, traditional, attraction models as antiquated and irrelevant.

It might be helpful to see the issue in terms of engineering and architecture. There has to be some observance of structural principles, but there has to be liberty to express creativity in the functional design.

### Sociological factors – church context

In discussing church growth and decline David Alan Roozen and Jackson Walker Carroll noted that church membership change did not occur because of one single

---

Dever, *Nine Marks of a Healthy Church* (Wheaton, IL: Crossway Books, 2000), and Stephen A. Macchia, *Becoming a Healthy Church: 10 Characteristics* (Grand Rapids, MI: Baker Books, 1999).

cause. Rather it was produced by "a complex pattern of multiple and often interacting factors."[14] In the book *Understanding Church Growth and Decline*, Dean Richard Hoge and David A. Roozen edited one of the first serious efforts to study the impact of contextual factors on church growth using modern research methodology.[15] The context of a church could influence church growth in positive and negative ways.

For example, in the Indian cultural context today the gospel has an egalitarian appeal to those who are of lower caste (such as the Adivasi) or, indeed, outcasts (Dalits). The ideals of liberty, equality and fraternity belong rightly to the gospel, though usually associated with the republican principles of the French Revolution. Whereas those who are in the higher echelons of the caste system (Brahmin) are not attracted to the gospel in such significant numbers. Whereas the former groups (Adivasi and Dalits) have much to gain in terms of dignity and status, the latter group (Brahmin) have no tangible social incentive and so the gospel is less attractive to them. Similar sociological forces may well have an influence on whether one is attracted to or repelled by the gospel. This may be evident in the rejection or retention of colonial forms of church. It is worthy of note that the kind of evangelical exclusivity of Western culture has not found

---

[14] David A. Roozen and Jackson W. Carroll, "Recent Trends in Church Membership and Participation: An Introduction," in *Understanding Church Growth and Decline: 1950-1978*, ed. Dean R. Hoge and David A. Roozen (New York: The Pilgrim Press, 1979), 39.

[15] Dean R. Hoge and David A. Roozen, eds., *Understanding Church Growth and Decline: 1950-1978* (New York: The Pilgrim Press, 1979).

fertile soil in India. The church there is almost universally prone to what Western evangelicals might call "syncretism".[16]

One of the first books that addressed "church health" was *How To Grow a Church: Conversations about Church Growth* written by Donald McGavran and Win Arn in 1973. The subject of church health was introduced briefly in chapter four, "Diagnosing Church Health." Responding to a question by Arn, McGavran noted that church health, "...is like a doctor diagnosing the sickness of a patient. Until he knows what the disease is, how can he prescribe a cure? Until the church diagnoses the difficulty, how can the problem be remedied?"[17]

In 1977, Charles Chaney and Ron Lewis commented on the analogy of medicine and church health by stating:

> In medical terms, a diagnosis is the determination of a disease by a comprehensive examination of the patient. Accurate diagnosis is the foundation of modern medicine. Proper treatment is only possible when the cause of an illness is known ... Comparable procedure is necessary to determine the growth health of a church.[18]

Chaney and Lewis proposed a number of tests to identify areas of growth-disease and growth-health, including, numerical growth and type of growth. The notion of growth has both quantitative and qualitative dimensions; the latter was not always emphasized. In his book, *Your Church Can Be*

---

[16] The sociological dimension is worthy of further investigation but falls outside the scope of this work.

[17] McGavran and Arn, 60.

[18] Charles L. Chaney and Ron S. Lewis, *Design for Church Growth* (Nashville, TN: Broadman Press, 1997), 87.

*Healthy* Peter Wagner expanded McGavran's and Arn's idea that church health meant the absence of disease.[19]

One of Wagner's axioms of church growth was a "church must not have a terminal disease."[20] Wagner noted that sometimes churches in changing communities declined. This happened when people in a new cultural group began replacing the previous majority group of another culture. When a community became more culturally diverse many of the older group moved to another location. At first the people in the older group commuted to the church but eventually joined other churches in their new communities. Churches in rural communities can decline simply because people leave the community for education or employment and fewer people take their place, so sociological factors are not unimportant.

While the perspective of church health being the absence of disease may be useful, this idea has several problems. First, a negative definition makes a poor definition. Leith Anderson noted, "...if we insist on defining health in terms of illness, we will be malady-centered" rather than health centered.[21] Second, the definition is derived from a sociological rather than a biblical viewpoint. A condition that a sociologist may consider terminal may not be when viewed from the perspective of God's power. Third, Wagner made little effort to connect the Bible with his diseases. A study of the letters to

---

[19] C. Peter Wagner, *Your Church Can Be Healthy*, Creative Leadership Series (Nashville,TN: Abingdon, 1979). This book was revised as *The Healthy Church: Avoiding and Curing the 9 Diseases that Can Afflict Any Church* (Ventura, CA: Regal Books, 1996).

[20] Wagner, *The Healthy Church*, 24.

[21] Leith Anderson, "Is This Body Healthy?" chap. in *A Church for the 21st Century* (Minneapolis, MN: Bethany House Publishers, 1992), 127-8.

the churches in the book of Revelation could provide a picture of church disease from a more spiritual perspective.

## A healthy Family

The late Murray Bowen popularized the application of systems theory to family therapy.[22] In summarizing family systems therapy, Jerry Corey and Jim Bitter wrote:

> The family systems perspective holds that individuals are best understood within the context of relationships and through assessing the interactions within an entire family ... It is revolutionary to conclude that the identified client's problem might be a symptom of how the system functions, not just a symptom of the individual's maladjustment, history, and psychosocial development ... The one central principle agreed upon by family therapy practitioners, regardless of their particular approach, is that the client is connected to living systems and that change in one part of the unit reverberates throughout other parts ... The family therapy perspective calls for a conceptual shift, for the family is viewed as a functioning unit that is more than the sum of the roles of its various members.[23]

Bowen's ideas have proved useful to understanding how churches operate. One of Bowen's students, Edwin Friedman, applied family systems theory to ecclesiastical institutions.[24]

---

[22] Murray Bowen, *Family Therapy in Clinical Practice* (Northvale, NJ: Jason Aronson, 1994).

[23] Gerald Corey, *Theory and Practice of Counseling and Psychotherapy*, 6th ed. (Belmont, CA: Wadsworth, 2001), 387.

[24] Edwin H. Friedman, *Generation to Generation: Family Process in Church and Synagogue* (New York, NY: The Guildford Press, 1985).

Steinke used family systems theory to develop a better understanding of church health.[25] Ronald Richardson also related Bowen's theory to church health in his book *Creating a Healthier Church*. He wrote, "One of the keys to functioning in a healthy manner as a church is for the leaders to look at the church as a system rather than as a collection of isolated people."[26]

From a family system perspective, people react differently to emotional situations according to their context. A lack of awareness of the church as a family system could cause a congregation in times of conflict to focus on symptoms rather than the more complex systemic issues. Richardson noted that two biological life forces interact within every congregation – the togetherness force and the individuality force. The togetherness force drove people to want to be connected to others within a church. The individuality force drove people to become their own unique persons.

For Richardson the biblical passage of 1 Corinthians 9-13 served as one example of how Paul sought to balance these two forces. On the one hand, Paul called for unity within the church while also emphasizing that there was "one body but many members."[27] There is diversity in the body of Christ. Unity is not uniformity and "interdependence" better describes the relationship of believers rather than "independence."

---

[25] Peter L. Steinke, How Your Church Family Works (Bethesda, MD: Alban Institute, 1993) and Healthy Congregations (Bethesda, MD: Alban Institute, 1996).

[26] Ronald Richardson, *Creating a Healthier Church: Family Systems Theory, Leadership, and Congregational Life* (Minneapolis, MN: Fortress Press, 1996), 26.

[27] Ibid., 62

Using scriptural examples throughout his book, Richardson demonstrated how family systems theory could benefit the church in terms of resolving conflict, understanding the dynamics of church life and in setting goals. Family systems theory provided a framework for understanding the dynamics within churches. While not directly derived from Scripture, the model expressed biblical concepts that could be useful in developing healthy churches.

## Church Models

Robert Logan believes, "Effective churches are healthy churches; healthy churches are growing churches–they make more and better disciples."[28] Through his own trial-and-error process of leading churches to growth, Robert E. Logan proposed ten principles for developing effective churches.[29] These are:

1. Visionary faith and prayer

2. Effective pastoral leadership

3. Culturally relevant philosophy of ministry

4. Celebrative and reflective worship

5. Holistic disciple-making

6. Expanding network of cell groups

7. Developing and resourcing leaders

8. Mobilizing believers according to spiritual gifts

---

[28] Robert E. Logan, *Beyond Church Growth: Action Plans for Developing a Dynamic Church* (Grand Rapids, MI: Fleming H. Revell, 1989), 17.

[29] Ibid., 23-206.

9. Appropriate and productive programing

10. Starting churches that reproduce

In 1977, Steven Macchia developed a list of ten characteristics of a healthy church.[30] These are:

1. God's empowering presence

2. God-exalting worship

3. Spiritual disciplines

4. A learning and growing community

5. A commitment to loving and caring relationships

6. Servant leadership development

7. An outward focus

8. Wise administration and accountability

9. Networking with the body of Christ

10. Stewardship and generosity

Macchia's research involved developing an intuitive list of healthy church principles based on one hundred church visits. He surveyed 1,899 "highly committed Christians" participating in his annual conferences. This enabled Macchia to rank the characteristics according to their degree of importance and relevance. It was based upon the participant's opinions about the desirable and effective attributes of healthy churches. Macchia developed survey instruments for measuring a church's health, suggestions for

---

[30] Stephen A. Macchia, Becoming a Healthy Church: 10 Characteristics, 23.

guiding church group discussion and additional scriptural references for the ten health characteristics.[31]

Leith Anderson, proposed six signs of a healthy church:

1. A church that glorified God.

2. A church that produced disciples who seriously sought to obey the commandments of God.

3. A church where members were involved in ministry based on their spiritual gifts

4. A church that is incarnational.

5. A church involved in evangelism - a church that assimilated new people into the life and leadership of the church.

6. A church that was open to change - a church that trusted God.[32]

**Scientific Studies**

Several survey instruments have been developed to measure church health. However, most developers of church health instruments have provided little or no evidence for reliability or validity. One exception was Christian Schwarz. In 1996 in his book *Natural Church Development*, he presented a novel method for studying church health. He

---

[31] Stephen Macchia, *Becoming a Healthy Church Workbook: A Dialogue, Assessment, and Planning Tool* (Grand Rapids, MI: Baker Books, 2001). Unfortunately, no information regarding the development of the instruments was provided. Also, the additional biblical references proved to be limited and without comment.

[32] Anderson, 125-42. Anderson did not explain how he developed his signs of a healthy church. At best Anderson provided only one scriptural reference per sign.

classified churches according to a quality index. In explaining his procedure, Schwarz wrote:

> There is an unspoken assumption in the church growth movement that "growing congregations" are automatically "good churches." But is this equation accurate? We can find a great variety of statements on this subject in church growth literature, but in the end they are no more than opinions and hunches. The reason is simply that while quantitative growth in a church (size as well as growth rate) could be measured with a certain degree of accuracy, a reliable procedure for measuring qualitative growth with objective, demonstrable criteria was not yet available.[33]

Seeking to solve this problem, Schwarz proposed a measure of church quality called the "quality index" (QI). This index was based on eight quality characteristics:

1. Empowering leadership – church leaders who concentrated on preparing others for Christian ministry.

2. Gift-oriented ministry where Christians served according to their gifts.

3. Passionate spirituality, i.e., a situation where members lived committed lives and practiced their faith with joy and enthusiasm.

4. Functional structures, i.e., an organization that easily responded to new situations.

5. Inspiring worship.

---

[33] Christian A. Schwarz, *Natural Church Development: A Guide*, 20.

6. Holistic small groups, i.e., groups that ministered to the needs of its members.

7. Need-oriented evangelism, i.e., evangelistic outreach based upon members who had the gift of evangelism.

8. Loving relationships, i.e., where church members sincerely supported each other through church-sponsored events both inside and outside the church.[34]

Schwarz' research was a serious statistical study but it has been critiqued.[35]

## Scripture

In an article entitled "Theology and the Healthy Church," Paul Robertson wrote, "The church that fails to let biblically based theological reflection inform her identity and practice risks the danger of either sinking or losing her way in the storms of life."[36] Scripture must be the primary reference for a definition of church health. It is important, therefore, to take account of the words of Jesus to the seven churches of Asia Minor, recorded in Revelation 2 and 3.

### Biblical Models of Healthy Churches

Several authors have developed lists of healthy church characteristics by studying churches found in the New

---

[34] Ibid., 22-37.

[35] John Ellas and Flavil Yeakley, review of *Natural Church Development*, by Christian A. Schwarz, *Journal of the American Society for Church Growth 10* (Spring 1999), 83-92.

[36] Paul E. Robertson, "Theology of the Healthy Church," *The Theological Educator: A Journal of Theology and Ministry 57* (Spring 1998): 45-52.

Testament. This is firmer ground than observational studies of contemporary churches; care must be exercised to ensure the selection of truly healthy churches. Ken Hemphill says:

As long as the church dealt with methods, models, and marketing strategies, the church would only be treating the symptoms of the illness that is robbing the church of its vitality.

Hemphill continued,

As long as we continue to talk about symptoms, we will persist in thinking we can heal the sickness with another new program, method, or model ... The critical issue is that the supernatural empowering of the church which occurs when the church dwells in right relationship with its Head, Jesus Christ.[37]

Numerical growth constitutes only part of the measure of a church. Maturational growth involving the deepening of relationships and the transformation of culture must be an indication of health. In light of the Great Commission, Hemphill defined church growth as occurring, "when the local church supernaturally and faithfully fulfills the Great Commission in its unique context and with a vision for the world."[38]

From his study of the church at Antioch, Ken Hemphill developed eight principles the church of God used then. He suggests the twenty-first century church ought to continue to use these same principles:

1. Supernatural power.

---

[37] Ken Hemphill, *The Antioch Effect: 8 Characteristics of Highly Effective Churches*, (Nashville, TN: Broadman & Holman Publishers, 1994), 10.

[38] Ibid., 13.

2. Christ-exalting worship.

3. God-centred prayer.

4. Servant leaders.

5. Kingdom family relationships.

6. God-sized vision.

7. Passion for the lost.

8. Maturation of believers.[39]

**Body of Christ**

Paul used the church as a body metaphor in 1 Corinthians 12:12-27 to teach three important church health principles. First, he emphasized a multiplicity of tasks where each member supported the work of the whole. Second, every member needed to be involved in the work of the church if the church was to function in a healthy way. Third, church members functioned according to their spiritual gifts and not according to vacancies in an organizational structure.

The question, "Who is our master?" constituted one of Rick Warren's three questions regarding church health.[40] Warren suggests that Jesus Christ must be the Lord of a church in order to be considered healthy. According to Warren, rule by tradition, personality, finances, programs,

---

[39] Hemphill, Ken. *The Antioch Effect: 8 Characteristics of Highly Effective Churches*. Nashville, TN: Broadman & Holman Publishers, 1994, 15-181.

[40] Warren, Rick. *The Purpose Driven Church: Growth without Compromising Your Message & Mission*. Grand Rapids, MI: Zondervan Publishing House, 1995, 71.

buildings, events and seekers - characterizes unhealthy churches.[41]

In his book *The Measure of a Church*, Gene Getz wrote that the mark of a mature church was not being an active church, a growing church, a soul-winning church, a missionary-minded church, a smooth-running church, a Spirit-filled church or a big church. Instead, Getz said the essential quality of a mature church was love.[42] A reading of the words of Jesus to the seven churches in Revelation corroborates this.

### Mission and Mandate

Rick Warren said that he stopped using the term "church growth" around 1986, "...because of things that he did not like about the church growth movement."[43] His reasons included, the incessant comparing of churches, the tendency to be more analytical than prescriptive and the inadequacy of numerical growth to gauge church heath. He said, "You don't judge an army's strength by how many people sit in the mess hall. You judge an army on the basis of how many people are trained and active on the front line."[44] In a chapter in his book, *The Purpose Driven Church*, entitled, "The Foundation of a Healthy Church," Warren said, "If you want to build a

---

[41] Ibid, 77-79.

[42] Gene Getz, *The Measure of a Church* (Glendale, CA: Regal Books, 1973), 18-20.

[43] Rick Warren, "Comprehensive Health Plan: To Lead a Healthy Church Takes More Than Technique," interview by Ed Rowell and Kevin Miller, Leadership XVIII, no. 3 (Summer 1997): 22. For a comprehensive treatment of the Great Commandment, see Victor Paul Furnish, The Love Commandment in the New Testament (Nashville, TN: Abingdon Press, 1972).

[44] Ibid

healthy, strong, and growing church you *must* spend time laying a solid foundation. This is done by clarifying in the minds of everyone involved why the church exists and what it's supposed to do."[45]

Warren centered the purpose of the church around five purposes or functions found in Acts 2:42-47, worship, evangelism, fellowship, discipleship and service.[46] He believes that church health results from a balance of the five purposes of the church. He emphasizes, "Health is a result of balance ... When a church emphasizes any one purpose to the neglect of others that produces imbalance–unhealth."[47]

### Healthy Church Characteristics

A healthy church is a Bible-believing church. A church understands its culture and context. A healthy church is one where the connectedness and uniqueness of each member is valued. A healthy church is a praying church, empowered by the Holy Spirit. A church equips its members for ministry, and evangelism. A healthy church is a loving, caring, worshiping, unified church. A healthy church will have exemplary leaders. It will be a disciple-making church with empowering leaders. It will be servant-led and visionary. A healthy church will facilitate opportunities for every member to explore, test and develop their gifting. It will seek to fulfil the Great Commission and live according to the Great Commandment. A healthy church is an authentic community that consists of the redeemed and transformed and as such is an agent of transformation under the controlling power of the Holy

---

[45] Warren, *The Purpose Driven Church*, 86.

[46] Ibid., 103-9.

[47] Warren, "Comprehensive Health Plan: To Lead a Healthy Church Takes More Than Technique," 22.

Spirit. In short, a healthy church is biblically based, spiritually dynamic, mission focused, and servant led. A biblical foundation (as distinct from a sociological perspective) for diagnosing the health of the church is essential.

## A Simple Biblical Model

Before turning to the words of Jesus to the seven churches of Asia Minor, it will be necessary to consider an interpretive approach to the book of Revelation. However, before doing that it will be helpful to look at the words of Luke recorded in Acts 2:42, "And they devoted themselves to the apostles' teaching and the fellowship, to the breaking of bread and the prayers." (Acts 2:42)[48] Here is a simple biblical model of a healthy church, albeit sparse in detail, which may be, supplemented from Revelation chapters 2 and 3 as well as other passages of Scripture.

Four activities are listed here. They are four elements, which characterized a Christian gathering in the early church. The Christian church is a guardian or custodian of the truth and needs to be diligent in proclaiming that truth without fear or favor. Many today desert the truth of Scripture and disown it because it does not suit them. We should note that the early disciples 'devoted' themselves to the apostles teaching. They are an example to us, as we too should be committed to understanding the instruction of God's Word

---

[48] It cannot be stated with certainty that the model of church identified in Acts 2:42 is intended to be a universal model for all churches in all times and places. One reason for asserting that it may have been normal then and there but not necessarily normative in the here and now is that it is also recorded in this chapter that believers sold their possessions and distributed the proceeds to the needy. This was undoubtedly influenced by their eschatological hope of the Lord's imminent return.

and earnest in applying it to our lives. John Stott says, 'the Holy Spirit opened a school in Jerusalem that day; its teachers were the apostles whom Jesus appointed; and there were 3,000 pupils in the kindergarten!'

We must not think that doctrine is dry or divisive. Our faith is not just a mystical experience that disdains theology. It is not just a shared experience. Our faith is based on a body of divinity that is apostolic and historic. The fullness of the Holy Spirit and a close adherence to doctrine are linked. The Holy Spirit is the spirit of truth. The early disciples did not say, "We have the Holy Spirit so we can dispense with all earthly teachers." On the contrary, they eagerly received instruction. The teaching of the apostles has come down to us in the form of Scripture. 'Devotion' to the apostles' teaching means submission to Scripture in all matters of faith and practice. A Spirit- filled church is a church that studies Scripture and submits itself to its teaching. The Spirit of God leads the people of God to submit to the word of God. These were not merely four characteristics by which the early church was distinguished. They are four characteristics by which any church may be evaluated.

### The Soul of the Church

Have you ever asked yourself what a true church is meant to be like? Here is the answer. It starts with teaching, which Calvin called the, 'soul of the church'. Wherever the pure voice of the gospel is heard and where there is growth through the Word there you have a healthy church. Here is something vital to which we need to devote ourselves. It is part of the developing life of the Christian. Imagine being a devoted football fan without watching or attending the games, knowing the club/team history, discussing their progress, defending their honor or wearing their colors. Too many Christians are fair-weather supporters when it comes to doctrine. The Word of God needs to be read, interpreted and obeyed. The Word of God gives light to direct us in our walk with God and nourishment to strengthen us throughout the journey. When we read it, we are comforted, encouraged and challenged. We need to read it regularly to derive the benefits and blessings it contains. Being devoted to the apostles teaching means more than hearing it expounded. It means more than being a devoted listener. The Word must be obediently applied. The apostles' doctrine forms the basis of fellowship and underpins true unity. When we are gathered together under one roof, this is union, not unity. God calls us to move beyond that into a deeper spirit of unity. Not uniformity. Unity allows for diversity. Doctrine provides the grounds for unity and stability within the church. It is the basis for fellowship. We are entrusted with the sacred duty of guarding the truth. The best way to be a custodian of the truth is to love it and to live it. If we do not love it and live it why would anybody else want it?

### True Fellowship

We are called into fellowship with Christ, to share in the life of his Son. The closer we get to Jesus the closer we want to be. Fellowship with others arises out of our fellowship with God. We are united in Christ to each other. We belong to Christ and to one another. Fellowship is like a bicycle wheel. The spokes are connected to the hub at the center and the rim at the circumference. Therefore, each Christian is joined to Christ, who is the center of our fellowship, and joined also to every other believer in the wider circle of fellowship. As individual Christians (spokes in the wheel), we are functioning properly when we retain contact with both Christ and Christians. Problems begin when a spoke comes adrift at either end.

No Christian was meant to go it alone. We need fellowship because of the pressures of the world and the opposition of Satan. We need to belong to a place of worship where God's Word is faithfully preached. If we stay away from fellowship our love for the Lord Jesus will soon cool off, just as a piece of coal separated from the fire and left on the hearth will soon cool off and eventually become cold and dead. Being in the company of keen Christians is like being in the center of a fire. When we are together (with Jesus in the center), our passion for God is kindled and a fire of love blazes in our hearts and this generates warm Christian fellowship. Satan loves to weaken the effectiveness of Christians by splitting them up into fighting factions. Devotion to fellowship is waning in our day as Christians move from one church to another like fleas hop from one body to another.

### Breaking Bread Together

First-century Christians were devoted to the breaking of bread. It is nice to share a meal with friends, but this is no ordinary meal. Jesus took bread and wine and used them as a picture of his body and blood. By breaking bread together, the disciples were doing what Jesus had asked. This is an ordinance instituted by Christ. He requested it before he died, in order that the disciples might remember him.

All believers are called to engage in this simple service that portrays profound truths. The Lord's Table is a simple but powerful visual aid. The grape and the grain both went through a crushing process as Jesus did at Calvary. The Lord's Table is not a means to salvation. It is not an altar of sacrifice. It is not a meaningless, formal ceremony. Communion is a time for looking back at the historical event of Calvary. Communion is a time for looking inward, a time of self-examination in the light of Scripture. Communion is a time for looking outward. It is a call for sinners to see the gospel in the symbols of Christ's death. Communion is a time for looking upward. Let us turn our eyes upon Jesus, who has risen and ascended to heaven. It is something we do, 'until he comes'. Jesus is coming and we will move from remembering to reunion. This is a personal memorial and to remember him we need to forget the things that would distract us. We should remember the Lord Jesus at this supper, as Spurgeon said, 'As the trust of your hearts, as the object of your gratitude, as the lord of your conduct, as the joy of your lives.' In the prints of the nails, Jesus has his own memorials of us. God delights in devoted disciples.

### Devotion to Prayer

Just how devoted are you to prayer? Do you regularly pray, at least once a day? Do you join with others in the church for prayer times each week? A well-attended prayer meeting is the sign of a healthy church. A poorly attended prayer meeting is the sign of a weak church. Yet in many churches today, few attend the regular prayer meetings. Do you see prayer as an optional extra to the spiritual life or do you see it as essential to spiritual vitality? In the first-century, church believers were dedicated to praying together. Prayer was an expression of their devotion to God. It was an external sign of their unity in vision and purpose. It seems to me that some people see the mid-week church meeting as an interruption to their social life or their leisure activity. They would prefer to stay at home and watch television. In truth such people are neither devoted fully to the Lord nor to the fellowship of the saints.

Here is some personal advice from a pastor. Firstly, do not enroll for an evening class which clashes with the designated time of the church prayer meeting. Secondly, when you buy the T.V. guide tear out the page (day of the week) for which the church prayer meeting is scheduled and throw it in the bin. Thirdly, make an entry in your diary for the prayer meeting. We need to stop making excuses and start praying. If this sounds overzealous to you then you are in poor spiritual health. Has it ever occurred to you that the sermons can improve, people can be saved and newcomers attracted to the church if you took prayer more seriously? Where can we begin? Make it a consistent prayer that God would give you a heart for prayer. Faithfully following the four activities listed in Acts 2:42 is a recipe for developing healthy churches.

# Finding an Interpretive Approach to Revelation

The Book of Revelation was written around A.D. 95 in Asia Minor by the apostle John, who, was on the island of Patmos, not far from the coast of Asia Minor.[49] "I, John, your brother and partner in the tribulation and the kingdom and the patient endurance that are in Jesus, was on the island called Patmos on account of the word of God and the testimony of Jesus." (Rev.1:9). This has traditionally been taken to mean that he had been exiled there as a martyr for his Christian faith. Some scholars, however, have suggested that it might have been a regular stop on a preaching circuit. Next, the author said, "I was in the Spirit on the Lord's day, and I heard behind me a loud voice like a trumpet (Rev.1:10), and this voice told him to write what he was about to see. Thus begins the revelation disclosed to him in voice and vision.

Ephesus was both the capital of the Roman province of Asia and one of the earliest centers of Christianity. The book next contains seven short letters of exhortation to the Christian churches in the seven leading cities of Asia Minor -- Ephesus (2.1-7), Smyrna (2.9-11), Pergamon (2.12-17), Thyatira (2.18-29), Sardis (3.1-6), Philadelphia (3.7-13) and Laodicea (3.14-22). This region would become a key area for the expansion of Christianity into the Roman Empire.

---

[49] Some dispute authorship and date of writing but there is general agreement that it was written around A.D. 95 in Asia Minor by the apostle John.

Revelation is one of the most fascinating books of the Bible. However, much debate surrounds the proper interpretation of this work. Is it a prophecy of future events yet to take place, or have the prophecies of this book been fulfilled?

## Popular Views

Two popular authors highlight the debate that continues today. In his best-selling series *Left Behind*, Tim LaHaye wrote a fictional account based on his theological understanding that the events of Revelation will occur in the future. Popular radio talk show host Hank Hanegraaff disagrees strongly with the theology underlying LaHaye's perspective. In his book *The Apocalypse Code*, Hanegraaff asserts that the events of Revelation were largely fulfilled in AD 70 with the fall of the destruction of Jerusalem. He criticizes theologians for taking a hyper-literal approach to Revelation.[50] This begs the question, how should the book of Revelation be interpreted?

## Four interpretive models

The issues at the center of the debate between LaHaye and Hanegraaff have been around for a considerable amount of time, predating these individuals. Throughout the history of the church, there have been a number of diverse views about how Revelation ought to be interpreted. There are essentially four distinct interpretive models: idealist, preterist, historicist, and futurist.

**The idealist** model asserts that Revelation describes in symbolic terms the battle throughout the ages between God and Satan and good against evil. **The preterist** model asserts that the events recorded in Revelation were largely fulfilled

---

[50] Hank Hanegraaff, *The Apocalypse Code* (Nashville: Thomas Nelson, 2007), 20.

with the destruction of Jerusalem and its Temple in AD 70. **The historicist** model asserts that Revelation comprises a symbolic account of church history commencing in the first-century AD. According to this view, the prophecies of Revelation are fulfilled in various historic events such as the fall of the Roman Empire, the Protestant Reformation, and the French Revolution. **The futurist** model asserts that Revelation predicts events that will take place in the future. These events include the rapture of the church, seven years of tribulation, and a millennial rule of Christ upon the earth.

These interpretive models are essentially different hermeneutical approaches to the text of Scripture insofar as they try to apply principles of interpretation.[51] The issue of which hermeneutical approach should be applied is important in the debate about how Revelation ought to be interpreted.

The idealist model asserts that Revelation is apocalyptic literature and as such, it should be interpreted allegorically. The preterist model views the book of Revelation as a symbolic account of events that occurred in AD 70. The historicist view interprets the events as symbolic of all Western church history. The futurist approach asserts that the book of Revelation should be interpreted in a literal manner, that is, the events of Revelation are scheduled to take place in

---

[51] These may be based on the historical-grammatical (conservative evangelical) or the historical-critical (liberal) methods. See Louis Berkhof, *Principles of Biblical Interpretation* (Grand Rapids, Michigan: Baker Book House, 1950, twenty-fourth printing, April 1994); Dan McCarthy and Charles Clayton, *Let the Reader Understand: A guide to Interpreting and Applying the Bible* (Wheaton, Illinois: BridgePoint, 1994); Walter C. Kaiser Jr. and Moisés Silva, *Introduction to Biblical Hermeneutics: The Search for Meaning* (Grand Rapids, Michigan: Zondervan, revised and expanded edition, 2007); R. C. Sproul, *Knowing Scripture* (Downers Grove, Illinois: Inter Varsity Press, 1977, third printing 1979).

the future. Each of these interpretive models needs to be explored a little further.

## The Idealist Approach

The idealist model uses the allegorical method to interpret Revelation. This approach to Revelation was initiated by Origen (AD 185-254), being further circulated by Augustine (AD 354-420). According to this approach, the events of Revelation are not connected to specific historical events. Thus, the imagery of Revelation presents the continuing battle throughout history of God against Satan and good against evil. In this epic drama the redeemed are persecuted and martyred by the forces of evil but will ultimately be vindicated by the victorious Lord whose sovereignty is made manifest in history.

William Milligan, a nineteenth century scholar has said, "While the Apocalypse thus embraces the whole period of the Christian dispensation, it sets before us within this period the action of great principles and not special incidents; we are not to look in the Apocalypse for special events, but for the exhibition of the principles which govern the history of both the world and the Church."[52] Robert Mounce summarizes the idealist view stating "Revelation is a theological poem presenting the ageless struggle between the kingdom of light and the kingdom of darkness. It is a philosophy of history wherein Christian forces are continuously meeting and conquering the demonic forces of evil."[53]

---

[52] William Milligan, *The Book of Revelation* (London: Hodder and Stoughton, 1889), 153-4.

[53] Robert Mounce, *The New International Commentary of the New Testament: The Book of Revelation* (Grand Rapids: William Eerdmans Publishing Company, 1977), 43.

Thus, symbols in the book are not connected to particular events but indicate motifs during the course of church history. The struggles in the book are thus interpreted as spiritual warfare displayed in the persecution of believers, or battles that have happened in history.

So the beast from the sea could be understood as satanically inspired political opposition to the church in any age. The beast from the land may be viewed as corrupt religion or paganism. The Babylonian whore is symbolic of the compromised church or seduction by the world. The bowls, trumpets and seals typify natural disasters such as famines and wars that take place as God implements his sovereign will in history. Calamities are manifestations of God's displeasure with sinful unrepentant humanity. God is ultimately triumphant.

### Strengths and Weaknesses

The strength of this interpretation is that it circumvents the difficulties of harmonizing passages with events in history. Furthermore, it allows that Revelation is germane and applicable for every era of church history.[54]

Nevertheless, there are some weaknesses associated with this view especially as it denies any particular historical fulfillment.[55] The opening verse of the book suggest future, imminent fulfillment, 'The revelation of Jesus Christ, which God gave him to show to his servants the things that must soon take place' (Rev.1:1). There is the danger in this view of engaging in *eis*egesis (reading our meaning **into** the text) rather than *ex*egesis (taking the meaning of what the author meant **out of** the text). Thus, the idealist approach tends to

---

[54] Leon Morris, *Tyndale New Testament Commentaries: Revelation* (Grand Rapids: William Eerdmans Publishing Company, 1987), 20.

[55] Robert Mounce, 43.

lead to arbitrary and subjective interpretations. Adherents of this view have frequently permitted contemporary cultural and socio-political issues to determine interpretation rather than seeking the author's intended meaning.[56] Merrill Tenney says:

> The idealist view ... assumes a "spiritual" interpretation, and allows no concrete significance whatever to figures that it employs. According to this viewpoint they are not merely symbolic of events and persons, as the historicist view contends; they are only abstract symbols of good and evil. They may be attached to any time or place, but like the characters of Pilgrim's Progress, represent qualities or trends. In interpretation, the Apocalypse may thus mean anything or nothing according to the whim of the interpreter.[57]

The historical-grammatical method of hermeneutics is an approach to biblical interpretation, which safeguards the original, intended meaning of the author. Ignoring such contextual issues is likely to lead to alternate interpretations that may even contradict the author's intended meaning.[58]

---

[56] Robert Thomas, *Revelation: An Exegetical Commentary* (Chicago: Moody Press, 1992), 31-2.

[57] Merrill Tenney, *Interpreting Revelation* (Grand Rapids: William Eerdmans Publishing Company, 1957), 146.

[58] Postmodern hermeneutics is a reader-centered approach that flagrantly violates the principles of the historical-grammatical approach and it has led to arbitrary and subjective individual and community interpretations.

## The Preterist Approach

The preterist model takes its name from Latin, *preter* meaning "past". There are two preterist perspectives: full preterism and partial preterism. Both views believe that the prophecies of the Olivet Discourse of Matthew 24 and Revelation were fulfilled in the first century with the fall of Jerusalem in AD 70. Thus, chapters 1-3 describe the conditions in the seven churches of Asia Minor prior to the Jewish war (AD 66-70). The remaining chapters of Revelation and Jesus' Olivet Discourse describe the fall of Jerusalem to the Romans.

The Full preterist asserts that all the prophecies of Revelation were fulfilled in AD 70 and that the current age is the eternal state, or the New Heavens and the New Earth. Partial preterist asserts that most of the prophecies of Revelation were fulfilled in the destruction of Jerusalem. However, they believe that chapters 20-22 refer to future events such as the future resurrection of believers and the second coming of Christ. Those who hold a partial preterist view consider full preterism heretical as it denies the second coming of Christ and teaches an unorthodox view of the resurrection.

Some church historians trace the roots of preterism to Jesuit priest Luis de Alcazar (1554-1613).[59] Alcazar's interpretation is thought to be a reaction to the Protestant historicist interpretation of Revelation, which identified the Pope as the Antichrist. However, some preterist contend that preterist teachings are found in the writings of the early church as early as the fourth century AD.[60]

---

[59] Steven Gregg, *Four Views of Revelation* (Nashville: Thomas Nelson Publishers, 1997), 39.

[60] Ibid.

The date of the composition of Revelation is a critical matter in the preterist view. As this approach alleges that Revelation foretells the destruction of Jerusalem, preterists holds to a pre-AD 70 date of writing. According to this view, John was writing specifically to the church of his day and had only its situation in mind. Thus, preterists state that the book of Revelation was written to encourage the saints to persevere under the persecution of the Roman Empire.

Preterists suggest several reasons to support this view. First, Jesus stated at the end of the Olivet Discourse, "Truly, I say to you, this generation will not pass away until all these things take place." (Matt. 24:34). If a generation were understood to refer to a period of forty years then the fall of Jerusalem would fit this time frame. Second, the account of the historian Josephus' concerning the fall of Jerusalem seems to coincide with the symbolism of Revelation in a number of ways. Third, this view would be directly germane to the author's contemporaries.

However, a careful critique of this view reveals that the events described in the Olivet Discourse and in Revelation 4-19 are different in some ways from the fall of Jerusalem. For example, Jesus described his return to Jerusalem this way: "For as the lightning comes from the east and shines as far as the west, so will be the coming of the Son of Man." (Matt. 24:27). Preterist say this refers to the Roman army's advance on Jerusalem. However, the Roman army advanced on Jerusalem from west to east, and their assault was not as a quick lightning strike. The Jewish war lasted for several years before Jerusalem was besieged, and the city fell after a lengthy siege.[61] Another argument against the preterists view is that the Roman general Titus did not set up an

---

[61] Tim LaHaye and Thomas Ice, ed., *The End Times Controversy* (Eugene, OR.: Harvest House Publishers, 2003), 377.

"abomination of desolation" (Matt. 24:15) in the Jerusalem Temple. Rather, he destroyed the Temple and burned it to the ground. Thus, it appears the preterist is required to allegorize or stretch the metaphors and symbols in order to find fulfillment of the prophecies in the fall of Jerusalem.

Another example of allegorical interpretation by the preterist is their interpretation of Revelation 7:4. John identifies a special group of prophets: the 144,000 from the "tribes of Israel." Preterist Hanegraaff states that this group represents the true bride of Christ and is referred to in Revelation 7:9 as 'a great multitude that no one could number, from every nation, from all tribes and peoples and languages'. That is, the 144,000 in verse 4, and the great multitude in verse 9 are the same people.[62] This seems inconsistent with the context of the chapter for a number of reasons. First, consistently in Scripture the phrase "tribes of Israel" literally refers to Jews. Second, John says there are 12,000 from each of the twelve tribes of Israel. This would be a peculiar way to describe the multitude of believers from all nations.[63] Third, the context shows John is speaking of two different groups: one on the earth (the 144,000 referenced in 7:1-3), and the great multitude in heaven before the throne (7:9). Thus, Hanegraaff seems to be allegorizing the text. Robert Mounce states:

> The major problem with the preterist position is that the decisive victory portrayed in the latter chapters of the Apocalypse was never achieved. It is difficult to believe that John envisioned anything less than the complete overthrow of Satan, the final destruction of evil, and the eternal reign on God. If

---

[62] Hanegraaff, 125.

[63] Unless one thinks of Israel in spiritual rather than racial terms.

this is not to be, then either the Seer was essentially wrong in the major thrust of his message or his work was so helplessly ambiguous that its first recipients were all led astray.[64]

Mounce and other New Testament scholars assert that the preterist view is inconsistent and indulges in allegorical interpretations to make the text suit a particular theological perspective.

The preterist position depends on a pre-AD 70 date of writing. However, the majority of New Testament scholars reckon the date of composition to be AD 95. If John had written this book post AD 70 it could not predict of the fall of Jerusalem as this event would have already occurred. Herein there is a problem with the preterist view.

However, preterists suggest there are some reasons to believe that Revelation was written before AD 70. John makes no mention of the destruction of the Jerusalem Temple. They contend that if he was writing after the event it seems odd that he did not mention such a momentous event. However, if Revelation was written a quarter of a century after the incident there seems to be no good reason for mentioning this historical event. Nevertheless, John does not mention either Christ's prophecy of the fall of the Temple (Matt. 24, Mk. 13, Lu 21) or the fulfillment of this prophecy. John is told to "measure the temple of God and the altar and those who worship there" (Rev.11:1). The preterists view

---

[64] Robert Mounce, *The New International Commentary of the New Testament: The Book of Revelation* (Grand Rapids: William Eerdmans Publishing Company, 1977), 42.

asserts that this suggests that the Temple was still standing during the composition of the book.[65]

The preterist view (especially partial preterism) is upheld by such eminent scholars as R. C. Sproul, Hank Hanegraaff, Kenneth Gentry, and the late David Chilton.

## The Historicist Approach

This interpretive model asserts that Revelation is an essentially symbolic depiction, which portrays the unfolding of history from the first century to the end of the age. Thus, the symbols in the apocalypse correspond to events in the history of Western Europe, including various popes, the Protestant Reformation, the French Revolution, and rulers such as Charlemagne. Most interpreters place the events of their day in the later chapters of Revelation.

Many advocates of this position view chapters 1-3 as seven epochs in church history. The breaking of the seals thus represents the fall of the Roman Empire (chapters 4-7). The Trumpet judgments symbolize the invasions of the Roman Empire by the Goths, Visigoths, Vandals, Huns, Saracens, and Turks (chapters 8-10). Protestant historicists of the Reformation era believed the pontiff to be the antichrist. Thus, the true church was exemplified in its struggle against Roman Catholicism (chapters 11-13). The bowl judgments typify God's sentence on the Catholic Church (Revelation 14-16), climaxing in the future overthrow of Catholicism described in chapters 17-19.[66]

---

[65] Evidence for the AD 95 date of writing will be presented in the futurist section.

[66] Steven Gregg, *Four Views of Revelation* (Nashville: Thomas Nelson Publishers, 1997), 31, 217, 309, 399.

This approach allows for a wide variety of interpretations as those who espouse this view are inclined to interpret the text through their contemporary context. Thus, many understood the culmination of the book would occur in their own generation. John Walvoord points to the lack of agreement among historicists, "As many as fifty different interpretations of the book of Revelation therefore evolve, depending on the time and circumstances of the expositor."[67] Moses Stuart raised this same concern in the early nineteenth century, "Hithertho, scarcely any two original and independent expositors have agreed, in respect to some points very important in their bearing upon the interpretation of the book."[68]

The historicist approach focuses almost entirely on the church in Western Europe, largely ignoring the East, and this fails to account for God's activity throughout Asia and the rest of the world. Thus, such a view would have little meaning for the first century church, which John was addressing. It is improbable that believers in Asia Minor could have understood Revelation according to such an interpretive model.

Numbered amongst adherents of the historicist view were such eminent figures as John Wycliffe, John Knox, William Tyndale, Martin Luther, John Calvin, Ulrich Zwingli, John Wesley, Jonathan Edwards, George Whitefield, Charles Finney, C. H. Spurgeon, and Matthew Henry. The historicist view became widely disseminated during the Reformation because it associated the pontiff with the beasts identified in

---

[67] John Walvoord, *The Revelation of Jesus Christ* (Chicago: Moody Press, 1966), 19.

[68] Moses Stuart, *A Commentary on the Apocalypse* (Edinburgh: Maclachlan, Stewart & Co., 1847), 35.

Revelation 13. However, the historicist view has waned since the beginning of the twentieth century.

### The Futurist Approach

With the decline in popularity and influence of the historicist view there has been resurgence (particularly from the beginning of the twentieth century onwards) of the futurist view. This interpretive model asserts that the events of the Olivet Discourse and Revelation chapters 4-22 will occur in the future. Those who hold this view divide the book of Revelation into three sections as indicated in 1:19: "Write therefore the things that you have seen, those that are and those that are to take place after this." Thus, chapter 1 describes the past, chapters 2-3 describe the present and the rest of the book describes future events.

The futurist approach to the interpretation of Revelation is essentially literal. Thus, chapters 4-19 refer to a period known as the seven-year tribulation.[69] During this time, God's judgments will be dispensed as revealed in the seals, trumpets, and bowls. Chapter 13 describes a literal future world empire headed by a political and religious leader represented by the two beasts. Chapter 17 depicts a harlot who epitomizes the church in apostasy. Chapter 19 refers to the second coming of Jesus as well as the cataclysmic battle of Armageddon to be succeeded by a literal thousand-year rule of Christ upon the earth in chapter 20. Chapters 21-22 describe the post millennium creation of a New Heaven and

---

[69] See Daniel 9:27.

a New Earth and the inauguration of the heavenly city upon the earth.[70]

Futurists argue that a consistently literal or plain interpretation ought to be applied in understanding the book of Revelation. This is the historical-grammatical approach of hermeneutics. Thus literal interpretation of the Bible means ascertaining the original intended meaning of the author. This involves the consistent application of grammatical rules in the original language(s) and respecting the cultural framework of the text. Literal interpretation does not discount figurative or symbolic language. As J. P. Lange stated:

> The literalist (so called) is not one who denies that figurative language, that symbols, are used in prophecy, nor does he deny that great spiritual truths are set forth therein; his position is, simply, that the prophecies are to be normally interpreted (i.e., according to the received laws of language) as any other utterances are interpreted – that which is manifestly figurative being so regarded.[71]

Charles Ryrie concurs:

> Symbols, figures of speech and types are all interpreted plainly in this method, and they are in no way contrary to literal interpretation. After all, the very existence of any meaning for a figure of speech depends on the reality of the literal meaning of the

---

[70] While Christian Publishing House does hold to the Futurist position, we would encourage Bible students to read the following article, Resurrection Hope - Where?

http://www.christianpublishers.org/resurrection-hope-where

[71] J. P. Lange, *Commentary of the Holy Scriptures: Revelation* (New York: Scribner's, 1872), 98, quoted in Charles Ryrie, *Dispensationalism* (Chicago: Moody Publishers, 2007), 91.

terms involved. Figures often make the meaning plainer, but it is the literal, normal, or plain meaning that they convey to the reader.[72]

However, figurative language does not justify allegorical interpretation.

Futurists assert that the literal interpretation of Revelation has its origins in the ancient church fathers. Certainly, features of this understanding (such as a future millennial kingdom) are found in the writings of Clement of Rome (AD 96), Justin Martyr (AD 100-165), Irenaeus (AD 115-202), Tertullian (AD 150-225) and others. Those who adhere to a futurist position suggest that the church fathers held to a literal interpretation of the book until Origen (AD 185-254) introduced allegorical interpretation. This was further popularized by Augustine (AD 354-430). Literal interpretation of Revelation is evident throughout the history of the church and has experienced resurgence in the modern era.

The futurist interpretive model is widely accepted among evangelical Christians today.

Dispensational theology is a prevalent form of the futurist view, which is promulgated by schools such as Dallas Theological Seminary and Moody Bible Institute. Theologians such as Charles Ryrie, John Walvoord, and Dwight Pentecost are renowned scholars in this field. Tim LaHaye made this theology popular in the late twentieth century with his end-times series of novels.

Regrettably, there have been and continue to be preachers who mistakenly apply the futurist approach to associate current events with the symbols in Revelation. Some

---

[72] Charles Ryrie, *Dispensationalism* (Chicago: Moody Publishers, 2007), 91.

have even been involved in making predictions about the precise date of Christ's second coming. Although such preachers may have a wide appeal, they do not properly represent a biblical futurist view.

### Criticism

Critics contend that the futurist view makes Revelation irrelevant to the original first century readers. Another criticism is that the book ought to be rightly understood as apocalyptic literature and as such should be interpreted allegorically or symbolically rather than literally.[73] Hank Hanegraaff states, 'Thus, when a Biblical writer uses a symbol or an allegory, we do violence to his intentions if we interpret it in a strictly literal manner.'[74]

### Date of Writing

The date of composition of the book of Revelation is an important matter in the discussion, especially between preterist and futurists. As already noted preterists argue for a pre-AD 70 date while futurists hold to a date of AD 95. There are several reasons for the later date.

First, Irenaeus, in his work *Against Heresies*, states that John wrote Revelation at the end of Emperor Domitian's

---

[73] Christian Publishing House Note: Interpreting symbolic and figurative language literally does not mean that we deny the symbolic and figurative sense. For example, Jesus likened himself to the figurative door of a figurative sheep. Was Jesus literally a door, i.e., what hangs on hinges? No. Were the people that Jesus referenced literally sheep that walk in a pasture? No. We interpret what the author meant by the symbolic or figurative language, and this is what we take literally. Jesus is a door in that it is only **through** him, his ransom, that Sheeplike ones can be saved.—Luke 12:32; John 10:7-11; 14:6

[74] Hanegraaff, 14.

reign, which ended in AD 96. Irenaeus was a disciple of Polycarp, who was a disciple of the Apostle John. He thus had a connection with a contemporary of the Apostle John.

Second, the conditions of the seven churches in Revelation appear to describe a second-generation church setting rather than that of a first-generation. For example, the Church of Ephesus (Rev.2:1-7) is charged with abandoning their first love and warned of the Nicolaitan heresy. If John had written Revelation in AD 65, it would have overlapped with Paul's letter to the Ephesians and Timothy. However, Paul makes no mention of either the loss of first love or the threat of the Nicolaitans. Ephesus was Paul's headquarters for three years, and Apollos served there along with Aquila and Priscilla. The church of Smyrna did not exist during Paul's ministry (AD 60-64) as recorded by Polycarp, the first bishop of the city. Laodicea (Rev.3:14-22) is rebuked for being wealthy and lukewarm. However, in his letter to the Colossians, Paul commends the church three times (2:2, 4:13, 16). It would likely take more than three years for the church to decline to the point that chapter three would state there to be no commendable aspect about it. In addition, an earthquake in AD 61 left the city in ruins for many years. Thus, it is unlikely that in a ruined condition John would describe them as rich.

Preterists who favor the AD 70 date pose the question, "Why doesn't John mention the fall of the Temple which occurred in AD 70?" Futurists respond that John wrote about future events, and the destruction of the temple was twenty-five years in the past. He also wrote to a Gentile audience in Asia Minor, which was far removed from Jerusalem. Preterists also point to the fact that the Temple is mentioned in chapter eleven. Futurists respond that although John mentions a temple in Revelation 11:1-2, this does not mean it exists at the time of his writing. In Daniel 9:26-27 and Ezekiel 40-48, both prophets describe the temple, but it was not in existence when they described a future temple in their writings.

What did Jesus mean when he said, "this generation will not pass away until all these things take place"? (Matt. 24:34). The common futurist response is that Jesus was stating that the future generation about which he was speaking would not pass away once "these things" had begun. In other words, the generation living amid the time of the events he predicted will not pass away until all is fulfilled.

## Conclusion

Revelation is a complex but intriguing book. Discussion regarding how it ought to be interpreted continues. Despite differences of opinion, there is significant agreement.[75] All views believe that God is sovereign in history. Except for full preterism and some forms of idealism, all believe in the literal (physical) return of Christ. All views believe in the resurrection from the dead. All believe there will be a future judgment. All believe in an eternal state in which believers will be with God, and unbelievers will be separated from him. All agree upon the importance of the study of prophecy and its edification for the body of Christ.

When I set out to write this work my intention was to understand the words of Jesus to the seven churches of Asia Minor in their context and to elicit their application for the church today. An essential presupposition in my approach is that the words of Scripture are both timeless and timely. In other words, they have a particular historical significance as well as a contemporary resonance. The words of the apostle Paul to Timothy must apply to this portion of Scripture too: 'All Scripture is breathed out by God and profitable for

---

[75] Norman Geisler and Ron Rhodes, *Conviction Without Compromise* (Eugene, OR.: Harvest House Publishers, 2008), 333.

teaching, for reproof, for correction, and for training in righteousness' (2 Tim. 3:16). Thus, I found myself addressing certain questions, "In what way are these words of Jesus to the church relevant now?" "How are they profitable for teaching?" "Is there some relevant rebuke here for Christians in the twenty-first century?" "In what way might the church today find correction by paying attention to these words?" How can believers be trained in righteousness through these words?" In short, how may these precious words of the Lord be applied to individual Christians and to local communities of believers? The aim is to explore them with a view to developing healthy churches. If this work contributes something to that end, I will be immensely thankful to the Lord.

# A Message to the Church in Ephesus

# Diagnosing the Health of the Church
## (Ephesus 2:1-7)

---

The 'Prologue' to the book of Revelation reveals that this is a prophetic book. It speaks of things that were yet to happen.[76] It is a message from the Alpha and Omega, the one who was and is and is to come. The seven golden lampstands are the seven churches of Asia Minor. The one walking amongst the seven churches is Jesus. The beloved apostle John had been exiled on the island of Patmos because of his commitment to the Word of God. He maintained a faithful testimony in spite of opposition and persecution. Imbued by the Holy Spirit on the Lord's Day he was instructed to write to the seven churches:

### Revelation 1:9-13

[9] I, John, your brother and partner in the tribulation and the kingdom and the patient endurance that are in Jesus, was on the island called Patmos on account of the word of God and the testimony of Jesus. [10] I was in the Spirit on the Lord's day, and I heard behind me a loud voice like a trumpet [11] saying, "Write what you see in a book and send it to the seven churches, to Ephesus and to Smyrna and to Pergamum and to Thyatira and to Sardis and to Philadelphia and to Laodicea."

[12] Then I turned to see the voice that was speaking to me, and on turning I saw seven golden lampstands, [13] and in the midst of the lampstands one like a son of man, clothed with a long robe and with a golden sash around his chest.

---

[76] See Introduction for a brief and simple overview of different interpretive models of the book of Revelation.

## Asia Minor

Asia Minor, a peninsula also called Anatolia, comprised all of the Asian part of Turkey. Today the people there speak Turkish. The seas surrounding Asia Minor are the Black Sea, the Aegean Sea and the Mediterranean Sea. Because Asia Minor is between Christian Europe and Asia, many different cultures have lived there. Remnants of these cultures are there today. Many great historical peoples, like the Hittites, Greeks, Persians, Armenians, Romans, Goths, Minoans, Byzantines, and Turks have lived in or occupied Asia Minor.

The Roman Empire had a province called Asia, which was in Asia Minor. Later people started to call the entire continent Asia, so the peninsula Asia was called Asia Minor (little Asia).

### Important Commercially

The first letter was addressed to the church located in the city of Ephesus. Ephesus was important in its day for several reasons. First, it was important commercially. Ephesus was located on the Castor River, just a few miles inland from the Aegean Sea. It was noted for its magnificent harbor, and ships came to Ephesus from all over the known world bringing their goods and their wealth. It was the richest city in Asia Minor at that time (around A.D. 95).

### Important Politically

Second, it was an important city politically. Because of past service to the Empire of Rome, Ephesus was granted the right to be a 'free city". This meant that they practiced self-government. At a time when many countries and cities in the region were ruled by the colonial authority of Rome, being an independent, autonomous, self-governing entity was a privilege not taken lightly. Ephesus was proud of its privileged political position.

### Important Religiously

Third, it was an important city religiously. Ephesus was the home of the temple of Diana (Roman), or Artemis (Greek). In its day, it was one of the Seven Wonders of the World. People came from everywhere to that temple. Diana was the goddess of sex and fertility. A hideous statue of a many-breasted woman represented her. This temple had many prostitutes and the way one worshiped Diana was to have sexual relations with a temple prostitute.

The temple also served as a repository for valuables and as such, it was a kind of bank. People brought their possessions there for safekeeping. It also served as a museum for fine art. Art from all over the world was housed in this ancient temple. Furthermore, it was a refuge (sanctuary) for criminals. If a lawbreaker could get to the temple, he would be safe from prosecution. Ephesus had a reputation (dating back to the 5th and 6th centuries B.C.) as a wicked place. One Greek philosopher from that period commented on its infamous notoriety: "No one could live in Ephesus without weeping over the immorality which he must see on every side."[77]

### Paul Sent with the Gospel

It was to this vile city that God sent the Apostle Paul (Acts 18:19-21; 19; 20:17-38). He preached there for two years and founded this church. While Paul was there, he

---

[77] Heraclitus of Ephesus (Ἡράκλειτος ὁ Ἐφέσιος, c. 535 – c. 475 B.C.) was a pre-Socratic Greek philosopher, a native of the Greek city Ephesus, Ionia, on the coast of Asia Minor.

wrote the books of first and second Corinthians (c. A.D 55) at the end of his three- year residency. Paul left Timothy in Ephesus for a period of time to help establish the church and to help resolve some serious leadership problems. Aquila, Priscilla, and Apollos all labored in the Ephesian church.— Acts 18.

### Active Church

This was an active church, serving in a wicked hour. By the time that the book of Revelation was written (A.D. 95), many years had passed since the founding of this church. Then the Lord came to them to speak about where they were spiritually and where he wanted them to be. He came to them with a message of comfort. They were reminded that he had them safely in his hand (2:1). He 'holds the seven stars in his right hand'. This speaks of the Lord's absolute control and sovereignty.

### A Wicked Hour and a Watchful Lord

In a society that was out of control morally and spiritually the Lord, let them know that he was in control. That same message is needed today. He reminded them that he was with them, observing them and sustaining them. The Lord is ever watchful over his church sustaining it by his grace and power. These seven letters reveal that the Lord had something personal to say to each of the churches. He came to this church in Ephesus and spoke about his presence among them. Jesus made some observations concerning this church.

## Commendation

He began his remarks by talking about all that was right with this church. The Lord let them know that he had seen all the good they were doing in his name. He came to them with precious words of commendation. He praised their service:

### Revelation 2:2-3

2 "'I know your works, your toil and your patient endurance, and how you cannot bear with those who are evil, but have tested those who call themselves apostles and are not, and found them to be false. 3 I know you are enduring patiently and bearing up for my name's sake, and you have not grown weary.

### Works, Toil, Patience

Jesus used three words to describe the activity of this church. First, he referred to their "works". This word speaks of the good things they had done. They had been working and Jesus had noticed their activity. Second, Jesus referred to their "toil". This speaks of intense labor coupled with trouble. It suggests that they were active at some personal expense and sacrifice. Third, the Lord referred to their "patient endurance". They were steadfast in spite of opposition. Whatever resistance, resentment, ridicule, rejection and persecution they encountered they continued to serve the Lord faithfully.

As Jesus began to speak to this church, he did so in glowing terms. He commended them for their works and their doctrinal purity. It appears that this was a very busy congregation. They were active with many ministries occupying their time. In verse 2, Jesus used three words to describe the business of this church. The word "works" refers to their accomplishments. This church had been used of the

Lord to do great things in the community. The word "labor" speaks of intense work involving toil and pain. The word "patience" implies that they carried out their works for the Lord in the midst of great persecution. The city around them hated them and the message they preached. Therefore, this was a working church.

This church was not a country club where the believers met to congratulate themselves on their salvation. A healthy church is one where the saints gather to worship and to be equipped for service. Then they go out to work for the glory of God in their homes, schools, communities and places of work. God did not save the redeemed for a life of ease. Rather he rescued a people to be active in his work. This begs the question: If Jesus were to appear in any given local congregation of believers today, would he be pleased with its works, labor, and patience?

### Separation

Jesus also commended them for their separation (v.2b); "...you cannot bear with those who are evil". Their lifestyles were in keeping with their holy calling and vocation in Christ. These people were living a separated lifestyle. It was most likely this fact that led to their persecution. They were not characterized or contaminated by the immorality that defined and defiled their society. They took a stand on the side of morality and they lived differently than the world around them. God still expects this from all of his children. He demands separation from this evil world:

### Ephesians 5:1-8

[1] Therefore be imitators of God, as beloved children. [2] And walk in love, as Christ loved us and gave himself up for us, a fragrant offering and sacrifice to God.

³ But sexual immorality and all impurity or covetousness must not even be named among you, as is proper among saints. ⁴ Let there be no filthiness nor foolish talk nor crude joking, which are out of place, but instead let there be thanksgiving. ⁵ For you may be sure of this, that everyone who is sexually immoral or impure, or who is covetous (that is, an idolater), has no inheritance in the kingdom of Christ and God. ⁶ Let no one deceive you with empty words, for because of these things the wrath of God comes upon the sons of disobedience. ⁷ Therefore do not become partners with them; ⁸ for at one time you were darkness, but now you are light in the Lord. Walk as children of light

This is a clarion call to holiness in walk, talk, dress (modest, irrespective of the fashion trends), choices of entertainment and so on. If Jesus were to speak to the church today, would he commend it for being a separated people? Followers of Christ are to be *in* the world but not *of* the world. In other words believers are occupants of this world but ought not to be occupied (or preoccupied) by it. That means not being influenced by its worldview and lifestyle. This is a missing note in today's church. Many Christians are scrambling to present themselves in a way that minimizes differences that should be emphasized. This is driven by a desire to be accepted or a fear of being rejected. The Christian is not, however, called to a monastic lifestyle, quarantined from the world in hallowed cloisters for fear of contamination. Every church community in contemporary culture must face the challenge of evangelism and engagement in meaningful but uncompromising ways.

## Stand and Standards (vs. 2, 6)

These people were praised because they held fast to correct doctrine. They tested the teaching of others. Heresy can only be identified for what it is if the truth is understood clearly. The best way of identifying counterfeit banknotes is not to study them for their differences but to be thoroughly familiar with the authentic article itself. The Ephesian believers checked out the credentials of others and they examined their teaching. If what they said did not line up with the Word of God, they refused to hear them, or to fellowship with them, but they exposed them to be the liars they were.

They were commended for their stand against the Nicolaitans. No one knows for sure who these people were, but there are a couple of possibilities. The word comes from two Greek words; *nikao* (to conquer) and *laos* (the people). Therefore, the Nicolaitans could have been a group of church leaders who wanted to control the people in a domineering way. Another possibility is that the Nicolaitans were followers of somebody named Nicolas who attempted to lead the people away from the Lord and into heresy and/or immorality. It is possible that he preached a doctrine that allowed people to serve the Lord and still lead immoral lives. The Ephesian believers refused to allow false doctrine to exist in their fellowship.

### Berean Model

How did they do this? They placed every teaching alongside the Word of God. If it did not line up with the book, they refused to receive it. That same attitude is needed today. Sadly, too many Christians believe everything they hear. There is nothing wrong with listening to sermons online but there are many sermon surfers, who are not as connected to local churches as they ought to be. They are feeding on a diet from celebrity preachers who have a cult following and their ideas for good or ill are infiltrating churches under the radar. The Berean believers put everything they heard to the test. Here is what the Bible says about them:

### Acts 17:10-11

[10] The brothers immediately sent Paul and Silas away by night to Berea, and when they arrived they went into the Jewish synagogue. [11] Now these Jews were more noble than those in Thessalonica; they received the word with all eagerness, examining the Scriptures daily to see if these things were so.[78]

The veracity of truth claims must be verified in Scripture.

### Steadfastness (v.3)

This church had been enduring opposition in an evil culture and laboring without any signs of weariness. They were steadfast. On the surface, the church at Ephesus is what every church should strive to be. The people of God should be busy for the Lord. This was the good advice from the apostle Paul to the Corinthian church: 'Therefore, my beloved brothers, be steadfast, immovable, always abounding in the work of the Lord, knowing that in the Lord your labor is not in vain.' (1 Cor. 15:58) Would Jesus commend us for our steadfastness?

---

[78] It must be acknowledged that the Bereans were not believers but their *modus operandi*, in checking the veracity of truth claims by using Scripture, is commendable.

## Complaint

Jesus exposed the reality of their situation. After offering this church some words of *commendation*, Jesus then spoke some words of *complaint*. The Lord expressed his disappointment. What a sad situation this is. While they looked good on the surface, there were problems in the heart that needed be dealt with. The Lord was grieved by the problems he saw in this church.

Jesus sees what Christians do, but he also sees who they are. He is able to look beneath the surface of people's lives and see the condition of hearts. When he finds lukewarm love it grieves him and it hinders the Christian's ability to enjoy God's blessing. If the Christian allows the wrong kind of things to linger in the heart, it grieves the Lord. Scripture cautions against giving offence to the Holy Spirit: 'And do not grieve the Holy Spirit of God.'—Ephesians 4:30.

## Diagnosis

The great physician of the soul examined the life and witness of this church. It should be borne in mind that this church like all churches consists of individual believers. Each one has a responsibility to submit himself regularly to the scrutiny of the Lord. This is not negative introspection but careful self-examination in the light of Scripture. Jesus looked at the people whom he loved and for whom he died and told them that they simply do not love him as they used to. He said, "you have abandoned the love you had at first". They still had love, but the quality of that love had diminished. That deep, fervent, burning love that once filled them with passion had cooled. They loved their church; but they did not love Jesus like they used to do. They loved their doctrine; but they had lost their passion for the Lord. They loved their work; but they were not motivated in that work by a passionate love for Jesus. They were busy, but their hearts no longer burned for him. The flame that had burned so hotly and brightly when it was first ignited had become merely a smoldering ember.

## A love Affair

The Christian life is basically a love affair with the Lord Jesus Christ. Being saved is falling in love with him. It begins with the quickening of the Holy Spirit, which induces a conviction of sinfulness that leads to repentance and faith. Growing in salvation is falling deeper in love with him. This love is the highest motive for all the believer does in his name. Works, witness, worship and service must all flow out of an ever-deepening love for Jesus. If the Christian loses that love for him, then service means nothing at all:

### 1 Corinthians 13:1-3

¹ If I speak in the tongues of men and of angels, but have not love, I am a noisy gong or a clanging cymbal. ² And if I have prophetic powers, and understand all mysteries and all knowledge, and if I have all faith, so as to remove mountains, but have not love, I am nothing. ³ If I give away all I have, and if I deliver up my body to be burned, but have not love, I gain nothing.

Love is a living, organic and dynamic thing. It is not meant to be static. Love is meant to grow. Love for Jesus can grow or just grow cold?

What is first love anyway? What makes it so special? First love is fervent. It is emotional. It moves the heart. It is vibrant and makes the one in love feel excited, hopeful, joyous and content (not complacent).

## Personal Illustration

First love is extravagant. The most important thing in my life as a young man was my record player. I loved music and I had a good stereo sound system. Then I fell in love with a beautiful young woman and I sold my stereo so that I could buy an engagement ring for her. I was glad to do it. She was worth everything to me and I wanted to marry her and spend the rest of my life with her. After three years of courtship and thirty-five years of marriage, I love her more now than ever.

## Mary and the Alabaster Jar

The Gospel account of Mary the disciple of Jesus with her alabaster box of ointment is instructive. It was an expensive perfume but she poured it all on the Lord. Others *condemned* her actions as extravagant but Jesus *commended* her for what she did. Every believer ought to love Jesus like this. Service for Christ ought to be conceived in love not from a loveless sense of duty. There is nothing wrong with a dutiful attitude, if it is motivated by love for the Lord. It is possible to labor without love; but it is impossible to love without labor.

## Martha

The church of Ephesus was active in the Lord's work, but it seems they were serving out of a sense of duty and not out of a fervent love for Christ. They had become like Martha (Luke 10:38-42). She labored, but not out of love. This is a challenge to every believer. Service may be conducted to fulfil the expectations of others rather than love for the Lord? Love for Jesus should be the basis of all Christian service: 'Whatever you do, work heartily, as for the Lord and not for men' (Colossians 3:23).

This is the litmus test. If Christians cannot honestly say that their hearts are still filled with that first, fervent, emotional, extravagant love for Jesus then it is time to take corrective action. Jesus desires reciprocal love. That means loving him with all the heart, soul, mind and strength (Mark 12:30). Such love is developed by the enabling power of the Holy Spirit.

## Three Perspectives

This is the first of seven letters written to different churches that existed in Asia Minor in the first century. These letters could be considered from three different perspectives.

First, they can be viewed *prophetically*, speaking of things yet to come.[79] This church in Ephesus existed in a period between the Day of Pentecost and A.D. 95. This was a time of great and rapid expansion for the early church. It was also a time of intense persecution. Some believers began to lose their zeal and fervency as the hope of Christ's imminent return waned.

Second, these letters can be viewed *practically*. They were sent to real congregations that were actually functioning at the close of the first century. While they were written to real churches existing in that day, they still speak to every church in existence today. The apostle Paul writing to Timothy said: 'All Scripture is breathed out by God and profitable for teaching, for reproof, for correction, and for training in righteousness, that the man of God may be competent, equipped for every good work' (2 Tim. 3:16-17).

---

[79] See Introduction which explores different theories concerning whether the events of Revelation had been fulfilled or partially fulfilled in A.D. 70 or were yet to occur. There is certainly a future eschatological dimension to the book of Revelation.

This begs some important questions. In what way are these letters in Revelation profitable? What teaching do they offer? Is there some reproof or correction to note? In what way do they facilitate training in righteousness? It may be noted that the end in mind is to equip the Christian for service by developing competencies that can be practically applied.

When Paul refers to 'Scripture' here, he is not merely referring to the Old Testament. The apostle Peter confirms this: 'Paul also wrote to you according to the wisdom given him, as he does in all his letters when he speaks in them of these matters. There are some things in them that are hard to understand, which the ignorant and unstable twist to their own destruction, as they do the other Scriptures' (2 Peter 3:15-16). The last phrase here, 'as they do the other Scriptures', indicates clearly that Peter considered the writings of Paul to be of equal status with the books of the Old Testament. In other words he deemed them to be inspired, inerrant and authoritative in all matters of faith and practice.

Third, these epistles can be viewed *personally*. These letters speak to congregations, but one needs to be mindful that the Lord has a word for the individual in these letters as well. He has something to say to Christians now. He has something to say about the quality of the believer's relationship with him.

### Doctrinal Purity

Verses 2-3 and verse 6 also indicate that this church was doctrinally pure. They stood for the truth and against evil. They publically exposed false prophets. They were not allowing the world to influence their worship or their walk. Anyone looking in from the outside would have concluded that they were a rock solid congregation. Anyone attending their services would have been in awe of their work and their calendar of activities. While those around them were looking at them, someone far more important had his eye on this church. The church is to bear witness to the Lord before a watching world, but it must always be conscious that the Lord beholds the thoughts, words and deeds of people. The Lord Jesus Christ was walking in their midst (verse 1) but they were unaware of his presence.

While they had much to commend them, there were problems in the church of Ephesus. The Lord knew what the people around them did not know. The Lord knew what the church itself did not know. The Lord knew that this church was just going through the motions of serving him. He knew that they did not love him as they had once loved him.

Considering the Lord's letter to this ancient congregation exposes the Christian church today to some uncomfortable questions about its true spiritual condition. As it was in Ephesus, many today are merely going through the motions. Many just do not love Jesus like they once did, and it shows.

### The Lord's Case against This Church (v.4)

After *commending* them for their works, Jesus *condemned* them for their lack of love for him. He told them that there was a real problem in their hearts. What is the nature of this problem?

### Personal Problem

This was a personal problem. Jesus said, "I have this against you". The Ephesians probably thought their biggest problems were the pagans around them and the persecution they faced. Jesus told them that the biggest problem they faced was a personal problem with the Lord himself. The Lord cares about his people. If he did not have his eye on them, he would have been unaware of their problem. Verse 1, says he walks among them. In verse 2, Jesus says, "I know". He knows his people far better than they know themselves. Nobody in the church of Ephesus would have guessed that there was a problem between them and Jesus, but there was.

Many Christians are smug and self-satisfied in their faith. The problem with gauging one's state of rightness is that one tends to make comparisons with others and rarely with others who live holier lives. Everybody wants to make favorable comparisons that present them in the best possible light. I have a few mirrors in my home and I confess (to my shame) that I prefer to look at myself in one particular mirror that is slightly tinted because it makes me look better than I really am. This is how it is morally. People want to view themselves in the most positive and advantageous way. God's standard of holiness is a lot higher than that. His standard of righteousness is Christ himself.

## A Passion Problem

Jesus told them exactly what they had done and failed to do to offend him. He said, "...you have abandoned the love you had at first". In other words, they just don't love him like they used to. They had not forsaken love altogether but they had neglected it. There was a cooling off in their passion for Christ. The word "first" means first in rank or importance. They still loved their church and doctrines. They still loved their activities and busy schedules. They still loved all they did. They just did not love Jesus more than these other things. He was not first and foremost in their affections.

Some might think that falling out of love with Jesus is a minor thing. Some might think it is something that happens to many people and that it is not such a big deal. Some might think it is normal or natural that there would be a cooling off in the area of love after a time. One could argue that such intensity and fervor is difficult or even impossible to sustain over a long period. Those who might advance such arguments fail to understand the application, which ought to be rightly derived from this letter to the church in Ephesus, that falling out of love with Jesus, is a serious issue and it grieves the Lord. When Christians do not love Jesus as they should, they are in violation of the greatest commandment: "And you shall love the Lord your God with all your heart and with all your soul and with all your mind and with all your strength." (Mark 12:30) If Christians are not in love with him, they will not love others, as he expect of them.

Love is a fruit of the Holy Spirit. (Gal. 5:22) Love for others is the work of God in the heart. (1 Jn. 4:7-12) When believers do not love Jesus, as they should, they will not have a desire to be with him. They will not hang on his every word. They will not miss him when they drift away from him. The nearest thing that humans can say is like the kind of love Jesus desires from the church (his bride) is honeymoon love.[80] This is love that rejoices in the fellowship and intimacy between bride and groom. It is a love that causes the bride to want to be with the object of her affections always. That is how it is for a new believer. In the Christian life, the honeymoon must never end.

Over time, love may fade and the desire to be around Jesus and his people may fade too. What is the problem? It can all be traced back to a loss of first love. A decline in the intensity and purity of love may be almost imperceptible at first but over time, it will begin to manifest itself in obvious ways. When the Christian does not love Jesus, as he should,

---

[80] This is not to be confused with sexual relations, but rather should be understood of the depth of love that is shared at this most precious time in a relationship.

he will not serve the Lord as fervently as the Lord desires. In fact, the Lord not only desires such love, he demands it and deserves it. Such a person professing faith in Christ may attend church, but he is superficial, merely ticking boxes and going through the motions. This is marking time rather than marching forward in the spiritual life.

A person might profess to be saved but never share his faith with the lost. A person might teach a class, preach a sermon, lead a prayer meeting, lead a Bible study, but there will always be something lacking without love. Fervent, emotional, extravagant love for Jesus will always manifest itself in active, public service for him. There is a danger of not loving Jesus, as he desires. Are Christians today consumed with love for him? Has the flame of passion become a dying ember? If so then there is a need to fan that flame into life again. Everybody knows the difference between love and something less than love. Everybody knows which honors Jesus the most. Jesus desires reciprocal love. That is a love that responds to his pure and perfect love. Human love will always be limited but it should not become less than it ought to be as far as is humanly possible. Christians should not have to feign love. It should be a natural response to the love of God: 'because God's love has been poured into our hearts through the Holy Spirit who has been given to us.' (Rom. 5:5) Expressions of love may be a spontaneous overflow of feeling or a conscious effort of the will.

## A Plan of Action

Having addressed their problem Jesus gives them a plan of action. This is one of the wonderful things about God's Word. It challenges, confronts and condemns certain thoughts, words, deeds. It shines a light on motives and the true condition of the human heart. But it never stops there.

The Lord always provides a way of putting things right. He told them how they can go about rekindling the flames of passion for him that once burned so brightly. How did Jesus do this?

### Remember

First, Jesus called on them to *remember*: "Remember therefore from where you have fallen" (v.5). It is clear that there has been a descent from a loftier elevation to a lower order of affection. The Lord called them to look back. They needed to remember a time when their love for him was powerful, all consuming and the most important thing in their lives. They needed to get back to that place again. The first step on this journey of ascent to the region of first love is to *remember*. However, what if love was never all that intense? What then? Jesus called these believers, and by implication and application believers in every generation and geographical location, to a standard of excellence in love. To recall a time when love for Jesus was better than it is right now is to admit backsliding. Whether or not that initial experience of overwhelming love ever existed, the call from Christ is the same. He wants his people to get to that place where their passion for him reflects his love for them.

The Ephesian believers were to remember those early days of salvation when their love of God was central to their very existence. They were to remember how it felt to be saved and to know that all their sins had been forgiven. They were to remember what it felt like to know that they were no longer dead in sin but had been made alive in Jesus. They were to remember the excitement that the Word of God brought to their hearts. The Word of God ought to arouse such a sense of expectancy. The believer can look to the Lord for direction, counsel, and affirmation through his Word. The search for significance and security find ultimate fulfillment in

Jesus. He is all the status people need. A bride rejoices to take the name of her husband and a husband takes great delight in the wholehearted love she bears for his name. It is a powerful symbol of the oneness that exists between them. Is it a joy for believers to bear Christ's noble name as Christians? Believers would do well to remember that moment of coming to faith and remember those early days of excitement and joy.

### Recapture

Christians need not just to recall, but also to *recapture* the excitement and emotion of those early days. Jesus wanted the Ephesian believers to reflect on what he did for them. He wanted them to look back to a time when their love for him motivated everything they did. It is possible to be saved so long that the thrill of those early days becomes a distant memory. Remembering what it was like to first come to Jesus and have the weight of sin lifted is the first step in recapturing the sense of liberation and joy that ought to fill the Christian soul. The believer's heart should be tender to Jesus. The Christian ought to take time to reflect on how it used to be and then compare such first love with how it is now. Who can honestly say that they are still head over heels in love with Jesus today? When a saint of God falls out of love with Jesus, they are in a backslidden condition. The Ephesians needed revival. The first step in revival is remembering.

### Repent

Second, the Lord called on them to *repent*. Once they remembered what he had done for them, they would see how far they had drifted away. When they remembered they would recognize their sins. The word "repent" refers to a change of mind that leads to a change of action. When they understood the true condition of their hearts, would they turn to the Lord and fall in love with him again? The greatest need of the church in this generation and every generation is to fall in love with Jesus once again. Before this can be done there has to be recognition that lack of love for him is a sin. All the things that the Christian has allowed to come between him and the Lord are idols. There is a real problem with people, who think they love Jesus enough. People who fall into that category certainly do not love him enough. By God's grace and enabling power the believer should strive to love Jesus better today than yesterday and better tomorrow than today. Christian love for the Lord should be climbing that upward spiral that leads ultimately to the eternal joy of being in his presence.

When Christians repent of sin and turn from a lack of love, God will fill them with his Spirit. Jesus told the people that they need to repent of the sin of not loving him, as they should. The same counsel needs to be heeded by the modern church today. It is so easy to allow other things to come before the Lord: leisure, work, even church work can displace God.

### Repeat

Third, Jesus called on them to *repeat*: "...do the works you did at first". That word "first" is the same as the word "first" in verse four. It speaks of that which is first in rank and importance. In other words, Jesus called them to return to the things that are most important. What is most important when it comes to relationship with him? The Lord's call here is for the Ephesian believers to return to the simple fundamentals of the faith. It is a call to return to the altars of prayer. It is a call to come back to the Word of God. It is a call to return to a place of worship. It is a call to obedience to his will. It is a call for the church to walk in holiness. Jesus is still calling the church to return to these basic foundational activities. If Christians do not seek him in prayer, feed on his Word, offer true heart worship, and walk in holiness and obedience then they do not love him properly. If believers do not do these things, they cannot expect the Lord to bless. Doing these things are signs of true love for God. If a church does not do these things, it cannot expect him to move in power among his people who gather in his name. The Lord will respond to the heartfelt and genuine love of his people by manifesting himself in ever-increasing power in their lives as individuals and in the lives of churches.

If Christians want to see souls saved they must fall in love with Jesus and let that love be seen. If Christians want the power of God in the church they must fall in love with Jesus and let him live through them every day. If Christians can recapture fervent, emotional, extravagant, first love for Jesus that is all that is needed. It would transform the *child* of God and the *church* of God. The Ephesian believers were told to start doing once again the things they used to do. That is the key for their revival and it is the key to all revival, getting back to the things that are of foremost importance in the spiritual life such as reading the Bible, praying, witnessing and testifying.

### A Challenge from Jesus

The Lord issued a challenge: "If not, I will come to you and remove your lampstand from its place, unless you repent." The only remedy is repentance. Where there is repentance, there will be restoration. In verse five, Jesus explained the remedy. Jesus had not come to *hurt* them; he came to *help* them. First, he offered a word of *commendation*. Then he offered a word of *complaint*.

## Correction

Then he spoke a word of *correction*. He told them how they could fix what is wrong in their church. Frankly, they were called to remember their first love and the height from which they had fallen. In other words, they were to understand the distance that now existed between them and Jesus. Somewhere along the journey, their relationship with the Lord had taken a turn that would ultimately lead to estrangement and apostasy. They had not arrived at that destination but they were on the road to it. They were called to repent. That means to stop going in the wrong direction, take corrective action and go in the right direction. Expressing first love would involve repeating the things that ought to be prioritized in the spiritual life. The stern warning from Jesus to the believer is that if they fail to do this the flickering light of their corporate witness, as a body of local believers will be snuffed out. In summary, they are called to remember, repent, repeat or be removed.

There was a disparity between their *reputation* and the *reality* of their spiritual life. How many people hide behind masks of respectability? The great physician *diagnosed* the health of the church and identified an issue that needed to be put right. Then he *prescribed* a remedy. This is good news. This temporal judgment can be avoided by following the doctor's advice.

It is clear from this letter to the church in Ephesus that Christians can lose their first love. They can become busy in the Lord's work out of duty rather than love. The challenge is to be filled with fervent, emotional, extravagant love for Jesus. The heart can grow cold to God. Christian zeal for the Lord can diminish. Every Christian church needs to conduct a spiritual audit to ascertain if it needs to remember, repent, repeat the first works, and return to first love.

# A Message to the Church in Smyrna

# A Fragrant Church

The city of Smyrna was located approximately thirty-five miles north of Ephesus. It was a prosperous city with a population of over one hundred thousand in John's day (c. A.D. 95). That location had been inhabited for over three thousand years and no one knows for sure who founded Smyrna or exactly when it was established. A massive earthquake destroyed the city a few years before the birth of Jesus, but it was rebuilt and thrived. It possessed a safe harbor, where ships from all over the world came to buy and sell goods. It was called 'The Crown City' because it was surrounded by hills that resembled a crown. It was also known as 'The Flower of Asia'. Smyrna was famous for its music and culture. When the city chose a motto to be imprinted on their coinage, they chose the phrase: 'First in Asia in size and beauty'.

## Myrrh

Several characteristics made the city special in its day. First, it was famous for the production of myrrh. This substance came from a shrub-like tree that produced a bitter gum. When the leaves of this tree were crushed, they exuded a very fragrant odor. Myrrh was used as a perfume by the living and an embalming agent for the dead. Myrrh was mentioned in association with the life and ministry of the Lord Jesus Christ. The Magi brought gifts of gold, frankincense and myrrh to the infant Jesus. (Matt. 2:11) Jesus was offered wine mixed with myrrh (as a painkiller) when he was on the cross but he did not take it. (Mk 15:23) Nicodemus brought myrrh to anoint the body of Jesus for burial (Jn. 19:39). The word myrrh means "bitter" and it came to be associated with suffering and death.

## A Planned, Religious and Free City

Among the other factors that made the city of Smyrna special is the fact that it was a planned city. Most cities of that day just evolved without design. Smyrna and its streets were planned down to the last detail. It was a very religious city with many temples dedicated to the pantheon of gods and goddesses they worshipped. There were temples dedicated to Zeus, Cybele, Asklepios, Apollo, and Aphrodite, among others. In fact, there was a street that was paved with gold that ran from the temple of Zeus to the temple of Cybele. How that was protected from plunder is anybody's guess! While pagan religions dominated the life of Smyrna, there was also a thriving Jewish community there.

Smyrna was a free city. That means that it was an autonomous, self-governing city. However, they were intensely loyal to Rome. On one occasion, the citizens of Smyrna stripped the very clothing off their backs and sent these garments, along with all the food they could muster, to Roman soldiers who were cold and hungry on the battlefield.

## A Crushed Church

In this beautiful, wealthy, pagan, and free city, there existed a struggling Christian community. The church in Smyrna was undergoing intense persecution. The Lord Jesus came to them with a word of comfort for their dark days. He told them that even though they appear to be so weak and so poor, they were, in fact, rich beyond imagination. There is a word of consolation here for everyone who has ever or will ever suffer for Christ's sake.

Smyrna was a crushed church. It is easy to see that this church was going through intense problems because of their testimony for the Lord Jesus. They were letting their light shine in a dark world and they were being persecuted for it. Jesus told them: that they would have "tribulation". The word means "pressure". It was used in that day to refer to crushing an object under the weight of very heavy stones. The etymology of the word is interesting. The word "tribulation" comes from the Latin word *tribulum*. It refers to the stone wheels that were used to crush wheat to separate the kernel from the husk. This church was paying the price for their allegiance to Jesus. The pressure was on and they were suffering.

The Lord knows and cares when his people suffer. Isaiah, speaking prophetically about the messiah said, 'he was *crushed* for our iniquities' (Isaiah 53:5 emphasis added by italics). It is worthy of note that the emblems of bread and wine used universally today to remember the Lord's death (in obedience to the Lord's command when he instituted this ordinance, at what is called The Last Supper) undergo a crushing process. Wheat must be crushed to make flour, which must in turn be baked in an oven. Therefore, too, Christians can undergo crushing experiences and endure the intense heat of affliction in the cauldron of life. This is particularly so in countries where Christians are persecuted for their faith. Likewise, the grape undergoes a process of crushing and fermentation. When the children of Israel returned from Babylonian captivity and confessed their sin, they also acknowledged that the Lord was aware of their suffering even in the distant past: "And you saw the affliction of our fathers in Egypt and heard their cry at the Red Sea."—Nehemiah 9:9.

The persecution experienced by the believers in Smyrna did not come only from the pagans in Smyrna. Verse nine reveals that they were also suffering at the hands of the Jews. The Jews in Smyrna joined with the idolaters in that city to defeat and destroy the Christians by whatever means necessary, just as the Pharisees and Herodians had united to kill Jesus. Jesus calls them "the synagogue of Satan" and accuses them of slander against these believers.

## False Accusations

Why did the people of Smyrna hate the believers so much? There are several reasons. First, the Jews and the pagans accused the Christians of cannibalism. Christians observed the ordinance of communion and part of that observance was eating the bread and drinking from the cup. These emblems represented the broken body and the shed blood of the Lord Jesus (1 Cor. 11:24-26). Clearly the meaning of the Lord's supper was either seriously misunderstood by those who interpreted this ordinance in a literal way (not allowing for metaphorical language in the words of Christ relating to these emblems) or it was grossly misrepresented by those who had a predisposed antipathy to Christians. Many Jews resented Christians because they were ushering in a new order that effectively disenfranchised the Jewish power base.

Second, when the Christians gathered, they would often hold what they called 'agape feasts.' These 'love feasts' were times of fellowship with one another but also a time of remembering the Lord with the bread and cup.

The pagans, however, accused the Christians of engaging in orgies, reflecting perhaps something of their own depravity.

Third, the Christians were hated because their beliefs and practices often split families. This was what Jesus said would happen (Matt. 10:34-36). Thus, Christians were accused of being anti-family.

Fourth, Christians were accused of being atheists because they did not worship the many gods of the pagans and because they used no statues and icons in their worship.[81] So, any natural disasters or other calamities were blamed on the Christians for incurring the wrath of the gods.

Fifth, Christians were accused of being political enemies of Rome because they refused to say: "Caesar is Lord!" Every Roman citizen was required to do this annually. To fail to do so brought severe punishment and even death.

### Poverty

Jesus said, "I know your tribulation and your poverty (but you are rich)". The word "poverty" speaks of being absolutely destitute. These poor people had nothing of this world's goods because of their relationship with the Lord Jesus. They were probably denied jobs and promotions because of their testimony. These people had nothing in a city that possessed everything.

### Prison

In verse ten, Jesus told them that there will be more trouble ahead. They will face more persecution. They were informed that "the devil is about to throw some of you into prison, that you may be tested, and for ten days". The "ten days" mentioned here might mean that their persecution would be severe, but brief. They are made aware that more

---

[81] Atheism in the ancient Greco-Roman world did not mean what it means today. In those days it referred to those who declined to worship the official/authorized 'gods'.

pain and suffering is coming their way, including imprisonment. Prison in that day was nothing like it is today. When people went to prison under the Roman system, they did not receive a college education, learn a skill and spend their days writing books and watching television. When a person went to prison in those days, it was often to await execution. When the death sentence was passed, it could be carried out in a number of different ways. One might be killed by a sword, burned alive, thrown to wild animals, or any of the dozens of other cruel methods of torture and torment they had devised. This was a suffering congregation which was about to undergo an even worse period of tribulation.

### The Martyrdom of Polycarp

One example of their suffering comes to us from history, some years after they received this letter. In A.D. 155, the bishop of the church of Smyrna, Polycarp, was martyred for Jesus. He possibly had known John, the apostle of Jesus and author of Revelation.[82] Polycarp was arrested at the request of an angry mob that cried: "Away with the atheists; let Polycarp be sought out!"[83] The old preacher was given the opportunity to renounce Jesus. The magistrate, who did not want to see the old man die, said, "What harm is there in saying, Lord Caesar?" However, Polycarp refused. When they entered the stadium, where the executions took place, they tried again saying: "Swear by the fortune of Caesar; repent,

---

[82] I am not dealing with issues of authorship here there are disagreements about which John wrote Revelation, not so much in the historical-grammatical tradition but rather in the historical-critical tradition of hermeneutics.

[83] In the ancient Greco-Roman world an atheist was a person who did not worship the official, authorised 'gods'.

and say, away with the atheists." Polycarp fixed his gaze on the crowd, waved his arms at *them* and said, "Away with the atheists!" The magistrate again attempted to get Polycarp to renounce his faith and said, "Swear, and I will set you at liberty, reproach Christ." To that, the old man cried out, "He never did me any injury: how then can I blaspheme my King and my Savior?" After a few more attempts to get him to renounce Jesus, they led him away to the stake and burned him alive. As the flames rose around him, he was heard to pray and rejoice in Jesus.

### Sharing in the Fellowship of Christ's Suffering

Everyone who will live a holy, separated, dedicated life for Jesus Christ, in any generation, will face persecution (2 Tim. 3:12). This should not be a surprise. Jesus said that it would be this way (Jn. 15:18-25; Mk. 13:13; Jn. 16:33). The reason the world hates the believer today is the same reason the world hated the believers then. They detest the unique and universal claims that Christians make concerning Christ. This cuts across their liberalism, pluralism, immorality and amorality. Christians who speak not only of heaven but also of hell, judgment and accountability are despised. The world has an aversion to believers because believers will not join in their abominations. In a world that reveres tolerance as the supreme virtue, Christians will be loathed because they are seen as intolerant.

### A Consistent Church

Smyrna was a *crushed* church but it was also a *consistent* church (v.9a). Even though they were paying a high price for their faithful love and service to the Lord Jesus, these people did not back away from their profession of faith. It would have been easy to do so. It must have been tempting. But they stayed the course and demonstrated a faithful testimony for the glory of God. Remember that Smyrna was famous for myrrh. It was only when the leaves of the tree were crushed that their fragrance was released. These people were being crushed under the terrible and terrifying pressure of persecution and they were releasing the fragrance of love and faithfulness to Jesus into the atmosphere of Smyrna.

## A Positive Testimony

Jesus sent seven letters to seven different churches. Five of the seven churches received words of rebuke and correction. Only this church and the church at Philadelphia received no corrective words. The Lord had been observing their walk and he was pleased. The church in Smyrna had a powerful testimony. Jesus said to them, "I know your works". In spite of all the darkness around them, these people continued to be a light for Jesus in the midst of an ever-darkening world. Their enemies did not intimidate them. They were not so frightened by the hatred of their opponents that they compromised. They proved they were genuine and that their faith was real by the way they conducted themselves in that society. Their testimony was powerful because they stayed the course and stuck to the task for the glory of God. In this, they were exemplary.

## Profession and Practice

In the present world, where darkness, wickedness and opposition to the Christian way of life abounds there is a tendency to back off the message, to tone things down. Within the walls of the church Christians are relatively safe from the critics and the enemies of truth. But believers cannot impact without confronting it. Believers need to step out of their comfort zones and into the world with the message of salvation. The apostle Paul said,

### Philippians 3:8-10

⁸ Indeed, I count everything as loss because of the surpassing worth of knowing Christ Jesus my Lord. For his sake I have suffered the loss of all things and count them as rubbish, in order that I may gain Christ ⁹ and be found in him, not having a righteousness of my own that comes from the law, but that which comes through faith in Christ, the righteousness from God that depends on faith— ¹⁰ that I may know him and the power of his resurrection, and may share his sufferings, becoming like him in his death,

What a bold statement. It was not just rhetoric. If a Christian church would be a powerful witness for the Lord Jesus then it must live out its profession, regardless of the personal or public cost.

### Comforted

Smyrna was a *crushed* and *consistent* church but it was *comforted* by Jesus. The Lord came to this beleaguered church and gave them a message of comfort they desperately needed to hear. Jesus said, "I know your works". The Lord of glory had taken a personal interest in the church in Smyrna. The word "know" means to know by experience. Jesus was saying, "I know you are having it tough; but you need to know that I am in this with you. I experience everything they do to you. When they do it to you, they do it to me." Was this not after all what Jesus said to Saul in his dramatic Damascus road encounter with the risen Christ? In that incident, Jesus said, "Saul, Saul, why are you persecuting *me*?" (Acts 9:4 emphasis added by italics). Jesus takes the persecution of his church very personally indeed. He wanted them to know that they were not alone in their struggle. He is always close to the suffering saint.

It is greatly encouraging to know that Jesus is with his people every step of the way (Hebrews 13:5). When they are ridiculed and rejected, he knows all about it because it touches him too: 'For we do not have a high priest who is unable to sympathize with our weaknesses' (Hebrews 4:15). He can help his people weather the storms and endure the pain. The Lord is involved in the suffering of believers. He is not a detached, distant and indifferent observer. Pain always has a purpose.

### Victory is Secured

When Jesus came to this church, he came as "the first and the last". He came as the one "which was dead, and is alive". Things might have appeared out of control, but they were in the hands of the Lord. Jesus is still sovereign. Jesus has been there. He told these saints that he knew what they are facing because he has already faced it. The people hated him. They persecuted him. They crucified him. But he ultimately prevailed. He has been through trials and emerged victorious. He is able to help his people when they face persecution and hatred. No matter what persecution the child of God encounters the Lord has already been there. He has already secured the victory. Surely, the believer can proclaim with confidence: 'If God is for us, who can be against us?' (Romans 8:31). The heavenly perspective in times of trial, testing and tribulation is summed up in Paul's letter to the Roman church:

### Romans 8:35-37

[35] Who shall separate us from the love of Christ? Shall tribulation, or distress, or persecution, or famine, or nakedness, or danger, or sword? [36] As it is written,

"For your sake we are being killed all the day long;
we are regarded as sheep to be slaughtered."

[37] No, in all these things we are more than conquerors through him who loved us.

### No Uncharted Waters

Thousands of years ago when men were beginning to take to the seas, their maps did not show the world as it is known today. They were only able to represent the places to which people had already sailed. In the places where men had never been before, in those unexplored, unknown areas, they would write on their maps: "Here be dragons". When Christians are voyaging on the seas of life and come into places that are new to them they may be certain that the captain of their salvation has gone before them. In such stormy and frightening seas, the believer can say with certainty, "Here is Jesus". There are no uncharted waters for the believer.

### Heavenly Treasure

Jesus said, "I know your tribulation and your poverty (but you are rich)". They may have lacked this world's goods, but their faith and the faithful display of their testimony was an investment in heaven. The incarnate Christ once said:

### Matthew 6:19-21

[19] "Do not lay up for yourselves treasures on earth, where moth and rust destroy and where thieves break in and steal,[20] but lay up for yourselves treasures in heaven, where neither moth nor rust destroys and where thieves do not break in and steal. [21] For where your treasure is, there your heart will be also.

These people had nothing, yet they possessed everything. (2 Cor. 6:10)

## Keeping What is Given Away

A certain wealthy believer had given away great sums of money over the years. When the stock market collapsed in the Great Depression, he lost the remainder of his resources and was left penniless. Someone asked him: "Are you sorry you gave away all that money?" The man answered: "Oh no! What I gave away is all I have left!" The Christian life is an investment in the Kingdom work of the Savior. The believers in Smyrna were investing in heaven but heaven was also investing in them. In fact heaven was their inheritance, not because of their suffering and poverty but because the Lord who was rich became poor for their sakes and suffered for their sins.

## A Victor's Crown

Believer may endure hell on earth for a while, but there will be no hell for them in eternity. The Lord promises them "a crown of life". That word for crown refers to the "*stephanos*" or the laurel crown that was given to victors in the ancient Greek games. This church looked like a bunch of losers to the world around them. In reality, they were mighty victors, waging spiritual warfare in the name of Jesus Christ. The day would come when they and their faith would be vindicated. There may be trials, tribulations, pain, and persecution but the followers of Jesus are on the road that will take them home to be with Jesus.

# A Message to the Church in Pergamum

# Carnal Church

The city of Pergamum was the capital city of Asia Minor. It was renowned for its political power, its intellectual achievement and its pagan worship. It was a wealthy city given over to luxury and fashion. There are two special features that caused Pergamum to stand out in its time.

## Library

First, there was a 200,000-volume library there. That may not sound like many books. But it is taken into consideration that every page of every book was handwritten on papyrus and parchment, it was quite an achievement. Pergamum was the place where parchment was invented. Parchment was a type of writing material developed from animal skins and far stronger than papyrus, which was made from reeds.

## Pagan temples

Second, a feature that marked ancient Pergamum was its pagan temples. There was a temple in Pergamum to Aesculapeus, the god of healing and medicine. His temple was filled with snakes and when a person needed healing, they would go into that temple, lie down on the floor and spend the night there. If a snake crawled across them during their stay, they considered themselves healed. There were three temples in Pergamum devoted to emperor cult worship. As already mentioned in the previous chapter Roman citizens were required to renew their vow by entering one of these temples, place a pinch of incense on an altar and say "Caesar is god". Christians who refused to do that were severely persecuted. On the hill outside the city there was a massive altar dedicated to Zeus, the supreme ruler of the gods. This altar was one hundred feet square, forty feet tall, and a dominant feature of that place.

## A Two-Edged Sword

It is to the Christian congregation in this city that Jesus addressed this letter. They were a church in desperate need of a word from the Lord. Therefore, when Jesus came to them, he came as one having the two-edged sword. The two-edged sword is a clear picture of the Word of God. Paul mentions this in his epistle to the Ephesians, '...the sword of the Spirit, which is the word of God' (Ephesians 6:12). The writer to the Hebrews also refers to the Word of God as a sword, 'For the word of God is living and active, sharper than any two-edged sword, piercing to the division of soul and of spirit, of joints and of marrow, and discerning the thoughts and intentions of the heart' (Heb. 4:12). The Lord came declaring that he had something to say to them.

## The Lord Knows

This church was doctrinally pure; but they had drifted into compromise. Jesus came to call them back to the right path. In these verses, there is a word for Christian hearts today. There is always the danger that believers might drift off center. There is the danger that believers might hold the right doctrines, but still drift into compromise with the world. Once again, Jesus said: "I know your works". The Lord knew all about this church, where it was, what it was doing and what it was facing. He knew them intimately. It is important to bear in mind that he knows his people and the churches to which they belong. Nothing is hidden from him.

He knows they are located in a place where there is fierce opposition. There are spiritual principalities and powers in the world and the church of Pergamum was situated in the very heart of Satan's evil empire, "where Satan's seat is... where Satan dwells." Pergamum was the throne room of satanic operations.

### A Cunning Adversary

This church existed in the middle of a city chosen by Satan as his headquarters on earth. Satan is not a red-scaly-skinned fiend who has a cloven foot, a spear-tipped tail and reeks of sulfur. He does not have horns and he does not carry a trident. That is a cartoon depiction or a Halloween costume. Satan is extremely intelligent, incredibly powerful and wicked beyond imagination. He is a cunning and subtle adversary of the Christian.

### Satan's Doom is Certain

Regardless of what some people think, some preachers preach and some songs say, Satan is not now, nor has he ever been in hell. He dreads that place more than any lost person ever has. When he is sent to hell, it will spell his eternal doom, and he knows it. Further on in the book of Revelation these words are recorded: '...and the devil who had deceived them was thrown into the lake of fire and sulfur where the beast and the false prophet were, and they will be tormented day and night forever and ever.'—Revelation 20:10.

### Satan is Active

Therefore, it is clear that Satan is not in hell and the apostle Peter corroborates this: 'the devil prowls around like a roaring lion, seeking someone to devour.' (1 Pet. 5:8). Therefore, today, Satan is free and he operates as the 'god of this world' (2 Cor. 4:4). In other words, Satan is active in the world and he has a seat of power somewhere. He is the prince of this world.—John 12:31; 14:30; 16:11.

### The Lord Knows and Cares

Jesus let the believers at Pergamum know that he knew they were living in a tough place. He knew their location and situation and he had a word just for them. He knows the situation of every Christian in every age. He knows when a believer is in a difficult marriage. He knows when they face persecution at work, at school, at home, or even in the church. He knows the pressures society places on the dedicated child of God. He knows. He cares. He is there and he will help.—Hebrews 13:5; 4:15-16.

### Not Ashamed

This church was not ashamed of the name of Jesus. His name is revered and reviled. His name is possibly the most divisive name in history. Yet his name is the only name whereby people can be saved (Ac 4:12). The church exists to promote Jesus. Jesus said, "And I, when I am lifted up from the earth, will draw all people to myself." Churches are to lift up the name of Jesus (Jn. 12:32) so that others might be drawn to him.

Jesus commended them because they had "not denied the faith." This church was doctrinally pure. They held on to the fundamentals of the faith, and Jesus praised them for it. There are some non-negotiable truths in Christianity. There is plenty of room for liberty in non-essentials. If a people do not hold certain things to be true, then they are not Christians, no matter what they say. This ancient church held fast to 'the faith' and in this they were exemplary.

## The Fundamentals of Faith

What are the fundamentals of faith? The Christian believes that salvation is by grace alone, through faith alone in Christ alone. He believes that the Scriptures as originally given are the inspired, inerrant and authoritative Word of God. The Christian believes in the vicarious death and victorious resurrection of the Savior. Believers need to take a stand on these precious truths. Far too many groups are turning away from the fundamental doctrines of the faith and are swiftly sliding into apostasy.

### Antipas

The Lord knew their situation and what it was costing them to stand for the faith. Even when this church was undergoing severe persecution, they stood for the Lord and for his Word. Jesus mentions a man by the name of Antipas. He is called a "faithful martyr". Antipas refused to offer the pinch of incense and say, "Caesar is god". Because of his refusal to worship Caesar, Antipas was placed inside a brass bull. A fire was built under the bull and Antipas was roasted to death. In spite of this, the Christians in Pergamum held fast to their witness. Jesus applauds them for their stand. Antipas has been virtually forgotten by history but Jesus knows his name and his sacrifice is not forgotten by the Lord.

### Ultimate Reward

Sacrifices for the Lord are never in vain. Jesus is aware of all the slights and hurts, cruel words and rejection, ridicule, pain, and sorrow that believers endure for his sake. The Lord will ultimately reward them openly. It is still costly to be a fundamental believer. Believers, who hold to the right doctrine and live the right kind of life, are going to offend some people and possibly face persecution. That is what

Scripture teaches: '...all who desire to live a godly life in Christ Jesus will be persecuted' (2 Tim. 3:12). When that happens, the Lord knows and he will reward faithful service in his time.

When the Savior looked at this church, he found some things that pleased him. However, sadly, not everything was to his liking. Here was a church that had fallen into a state of compromise with the world. They held onto pure doctrine but they embraced the world and Jesus confronted them about it. Here is what he says is wrong with this church. There is corruption in the membership (v.14). He confronted them because some of them "hold the doctrine of Balaam".

### Balaam

Balaam is one of the strangest characters in the pages of the Bible. On the one hand, he was a man intimately acquainted with God. He knew about God, about God's character and he even talked with God. On the other hand, he was motivated by greed and he was guilty of leading the people of God into immorality and idolatry.

His story can be found in Numbers 22-25. In those verses, Balak, the king of Moab, wanted to curse the nation of Israel, so he called for Balaam to come do the dirty work. He promised him wealth and promotion for his services. Four times Balaam tried to curse Israel, each time the Lord turned his curses into blessings. When he saw that his attempts to curse Israel had failed, Balaam apparently suggested that since they can't *curse* Israel, they should *corrupt* them. This was accomplished by leading them off into immorality and idolatry and thus bringing the wrath of God down upon them (Num. 25:1; 31:16). Balaam died by the sword.

## Worldliness

The "doctrine of Balaam" is wickedness and worldliness. The church at Pergamum was tolerating people in their midst who claimed to be Christians, but who lived like the world around them. Some of their membership were living immoral lives and participating in pagan worship. Jesus was not at all pleased with these things.

This same problem is rampant in the church today. There are many carnal Christians. There are so many who believe that since they are saved by grace and kept by grace, they can live any way they please. It is no wonder that society has no respect for the church. It is no wonder that there is no power in the church if Christians live as they please without regard for the clear commands of the Lord.

## The Heart of the Matter

Here is the fact of the matter: if a person is saved he will not be like the world around him. If a person is saved he will walk differently, talk differently, and have a different set of standards than the world. A Christian has different values and a different worldview. A Christian has different ambitions and desires. His first desire is to please the Lord. A Christian has different priorities and a different perspective. When Jesus saves a soul he creates a new creature (2 Cor. 5:17). He changes everything about that saved person's life. Yes the Christian still commits sin (1 John 1:8) but if confesses he is forgiven (1 Jn. 1:9). However, the Christian does not habitually commit sin. A Christian is different and this shows in the way he lives his life.

### Proving Christian Identity

There are some clear standards for living contained in the Bible. Believers can either live by them, thereby proving they are children of the light, or they can ignore them thereby proving they are children of darkness. But believers can't have it both ways.

Jesus told them to "repent". This word means to change the mind. Repentance is really a change of mind that results in a change of direction. If they refuse to repent and deal with the corruption and confusion in their midst he is going to fight against those who willfully and continuously indulge in such unacceptable practices. He is talking about people within the church. The Lord knows who belongs to him and who does not. Those who will not repent are going to have to face the Lord in judgment. It is a fearful thing to be found on the wrong side of the Lord. It is dangerous business to cause trouble in the church.

The Lord loves his church. He loves her so much that he died to redeem her. What man would stand by while his wife's integrity was being undermined? What kind of husband would allow his wife to be attacked, either verbally or physically? Any decent man would take his wife's part and defend her. Jesus Christ will not tolerate those who seek to corrupt his bride.

### Precious Promises

The Lord made some precious promises to the overcomers in the church. Those who walk with him in spite of dangers and defections can expect some precious things from his hand. Jesus promised special provisions. He promised them "hidden manna".

In the Old Testament, when the children of Israel wandered through the wilderness, God fed them by sending manna down from heaven. This manna is a picture of God's precious promise to feed his children.

## Satisfied with Jesus

The saints of God might be excluded from many things in this world but the Lord will feed them with delicacies the world cannot imagine or duplicate. He has some secret things hidden away just for his children. The true saint of God is content to be alone with his Lord feeding on his Word and his presence. Jesus promises his people a place of escape and refreshment, even during the most difficult of times.

## A White Stone

The Lord promised to give his faithful ones a white stone. This does not mean much today but it held special meaning to the people of that day. There are several possible meanings attached to the white stone.

### Innocent Verdict

White and black stones were used to indicate judgment in ancient courts of law. When a judge rendered his verdict, he would place a stone in a container and at the appropriate time, he would roll the stone out, thus rendering his judgment. A black stone indicated a judgment of guilt, while a white stone indicated a judgment of innocence. Jesus was telling these people that they might be blackballed by the world, but they were innocent in his eyes. He had taken all the black stones that were against them and he washed them white in his blood.

### Citizenship

White stones were used to signify citizenship. A white stone was often given to people who had proven their allegiance to the city. Jesus honors those who live for him.

### Victory

White stones were used as a symbol of victory. They were given to those who had won a victory in one of the ancient games. These white stones were called *tessera* and they allowed the owner free access to all public entertainment. Jesus allows his victors access to the glories of heaven. A courageous gladiator would be given a white stone with 'SP.' engraved on it. This stood for *spectatus*, which meant 'his valor had been proven beyond all doubt'. Therefore, Jesus promises to honor those who take a stand for him.

### Friendship

White stones were a symbol of friendship. Often two friends would take a white stone, break it in half and write the other friends name on their half. When they met, even after many years, they could place the halves of their stones together, signifying their lasting relationship.

### Access

White stones were used to gain access. When a wealthy person threw a party, they sometimes gave their invited guests a white stone. When it came time for the celebration, the person who presented a white stone was granted access to the banquet. Jesus allows his people access to the greatest banquet of all: the marriage supper of the Lamb (Revelation 19).

## Intimacy

Jesus promised his overcomers that their white stone would contain a new name. This was a promise of intimacy. It was customary in that day for guests at a dinner to have a white stone placed at their seat. When they were seated, they could look at the stone and underneath would be a private message from the host. It was a way for the host to share an intimate thought with each guest. Jesus promised those who were faithful to him that he would reveal himself to them in a personal, intimate way.

## Special Relationship

Each Christian has a unique and very special relationship with Jesus. I have a relationship with Jesus that others cannot have and others have a relationship with him that I cannot have. Believers are all saved the same way (by grace, through faith) but he has done things *in*, *for* and *to* me that he has not done *in for* and *to* others and *vice versa*. Every Christian has a special relationship. The Christian must ask if his relationship with Jesus is all that it should be. The Christian must ask if he professes to know Jesus even while he is living for the world.

# A Message to the Church in Thyatira

# A Compromised Church

---

Thyatira was the smallest of the seven cities mentioned in the letters to the churches. It is also the city about which the least is known. Yet, it was to this little-known church in a little-known city that Christ addressed his longest letter. While not a lot is known about ancient Thyatira, some things are known and they are worthy of mention.

### A Military Buffer Zone

Alexander the Great probably founded Thyatira about three hundred years before Christ. The name Thyatira means 'unceasing sacrifice'. It probably received this name because it was a military buffer city. It was located about forty miles southeast of Pergamum, the capital city of that province. When enemies invaded, they would naturally come to Thyatira first. While its location did not allow it to defend itself very well, its mission was to hold the enemy just long enough for Pergamum to prepare itself for battle. As a result, Thyatira was destroyed and rebuilt many times during its history.

### Commerce

It was somewhat famous in its day for commerce. There was a main trade route that went through the city. Thus, tradesmen from around the world bought and sold there. Thyatira was known for its woolen industry, especially for the dyes produced there. They manufactured a very expensive purple dye that was valued by royalty and the wealthy of that era. This dye was obtained from a certain shellfish. Divers brought up this little creature, it was cut open, and a single drop of this dye was obtained. That dye, coupled with the chemical composition of the water of Thyatira, made colors possible there that could not be reproduced anywhere else. This industry is mentioned in the Bible where a woman named Lydia who is called 'a seller of purple, of the city of Thyatira.—'Acts 16:14.

### Trade Guilds

Thyatira was also known for its trade guilds. These were like the ancient workers unions of the day. Workers from the various industries of the city such as bakers, wool workers, dyers, bronze workers, potters, and others banded together to set prices and guarantee the quality of their workmanship. To refuse to join a guild was to give up all prospects of work.

### Occult Worship

Thyatira was also a center of occult worship. There was a temple in the city dedicated to fortune telling. It was presided over by a female oracle named Sambathe.

### Confounded by a Woman

It was to the church operating in this city that Jesus sent this letter. It is not known who founded this church. It is possible that the Gospel was brought to Thyatira by Lydia who came to faith in Christ in Philippi. (Ac 16:12-15) Alternatively, as some think, believers from Ephesus might have evangelized it. One thing is certain. While the church in Thyatira might or might not have been *founded* by a woman, a woman was certainly *confounding* it.

There were serious problems in the church of Thyatira and the Lord came with a word tailored just for them and their need. Jesus presented himself to this church in several ways. He came as the saving one "the Son of God". He reminded these people that he is the Savior and that he alone is worthy of worship. He came as the searching one with "eyes like unto a flame of fire". He came as one who sees all. He can see the works of the hands and the motives and thoughts of the heart. He came, not as the meek and lowly Jesus, but with eyes ablaze with anger over sin. He came as the sovereign one with "feet like fine brass". Brass or bronze in the Bible is symbolic of judgment. Jesus not only came as one able to see all, he also came as one able to judge all.

### Compromised Church

This is a compromised church. Some people in this church were backslidden and their lifestyles were damaging the reputation of the church. Jesus commended the service of the church (v.19). This was an active church and it was commended for the fact that its current activity exceeded what it was in the past. They seem to have been well motivated. It is good that this church had love, but it is not certain that their works arose out of genuine love for the Lord. It seems that their love was centered on man and not on God.

### Faithful or Fickle

In some ways, they were faithful and not fickle. Jesus praised them for the level of maturity they had attained. Every church should be a busy for the glory of God. There is no excuse for not being active in the Lord's work. The church should be involved in exalting the Savior, edifying the saints, and evangelizing the sinner. These three tasks comprise the whole business of the church and Christians should be actively engaged in them for the glory of God.

### Confronted by Christ

Jesus commended the church in Thyatira for their service but he confronted them for their sin. On the surface, this church appeared to be everything a church ought to be. But it was corrupt at its core. The church in Thyatira was being led away from the Lord by the teachings of an influential woman in their congregation. The Lord confronted the teacher of this church.

It is an awesome responsibility to teach a congregation of believers and those who do so will be held accountable. James says, 'Not many of you should become teachers, my brothers, for you know that we who teach will be judged with greater strictness.'—James 3:1.

### Jezebel

This female teacher is called Jezebel. She is called by the name of one of the most infamous women in Scripture. The Old Testament character, Jezebel, was the wife of wicked king Ahab (1 Ki. 16:31). Ironically, her name means 'chaste' but she was anything but that. She was the wicked daughter of a Gentile king who was a devoted worshiper of the god Baal. She supported eight hundred and fifty prophets of that evil, sensual religion.—1 Kings 18:19.

Baal was a fertility god and his prophets and priests were no more than temple prostitutes. Baal was worshiped through vile sexual acts and gross wickedness. When Jezebel came to Israel, she brought her perverted religion with her. She led her husband to follow her gods and thus influenced Israel to seek Baal instead of Jehovah. (1 Ki. 21:25) She even did her best to kill every true man of God she could get her hands on. She threatened Elijah and he fled in fear.—1 Kings 19:1-3.

## Judgment

Scripture records the story of Ahab and his desire for Naboth's vineyard (1 Kings 21:1-29). It was Jezebel that arranged for the murder of Naboth so that Ahab could have the vineyard. This act prompted Elijah to pronounce God's sentence upon Ahab and Jezebel (1 Kings 21:17-24). He told Ahab that Jezebel would be eaten by the dogs (1 Kings 21:23). This was literally fulfilled years later when Jehu commanded Jezebel's servants to throw her down from a second floor window. They did and Jehu drove his chariot over her body. He went into the house, had a meal and commanded the servants to bury her. When they went out to retrieve her body, all that was left was her skull, her feet and the palms of her hands. The dogs had eaten the rest (2 Ki. 9:1-37). The name Jezebel came to be identified with wickedness and idol worship.

## Leading People Astray

The Jezebel mentioned in this section of the book of Revelation is, obviously, a different character to the Old Testament Jezebel. Her sin is described in verse 20. This prophetess, whoever she was, was guilty of leading the people away from the true worship of God.

The trade guilds would often have meetings in the pagan temples around town. Such meetings were often immoral affairs involving drunkenness and sexual immorality. These meetings would also involve a meal and would either begin or end with a sacrifice to a pagan god. When an animal was sacrificed in a pagan temple, often only a small portion was actually sacrificed. Sometimes, just some hair clipped from the head of the animal might be all that was used. The rest of the animal was then divided between the pagan priest and the worshipers. A worshiper could either sell his portion of the meat in the marketplace, or he could have a meal with his friends and they would eat the sacrifice.

When the pagans in Thyatira were saved, they were faced with a problem. Did they refuse to join the guilds and be unemployed? Or did they participate in the pagan rituals and compromise their testimony?

## Abstinence

The mind of God in this matter is found in the Jerusalem Council's letter to Gentile believers: '...abstain from what has been sacrificed to idols, and from blood, and from what has been strangled, and from sexual immorality. If you keep yourselves from these, you will do well' (Ac 15:29). There, newly converted Gentiles were commanded to abstain from meat sacrificed to idols and from sexual immorality.[84]

The teaching at Thyatira may have been the same teaching that was rampant in that era. That an individual could be saved by grace and indulge the fleshly appetite for sin. Some people held the view that the soul and the flesh were not connected. They taught that what a person did in their body had no effect on their spiritual life. This teaching is addressed and countered in the first epistle of John.

This woman preacher may have been telling the people in this church that they could hold onto their pagan beliefs and practices and still serve the Lord. This may have been the tool that church was using, which got the pagans of Thyatira to come to their church. They were compromising their standards to attract the world.

---

[84] For more information concerning eating meat sacrificed to idols see 1 Corinthians 8-10.

### Belief, Belonging and Behavior

This trend is back (if it ever went away) and it is becoming increasingly manifest in the notion that one can belong to a church irrespective of belief or behavior. This is motivated by the desire to be relevant and often promoted by genuine believers, especially overzealous but misguided evangelists. Whatever she was doing, she was leading the people of God astray.

The word "seduce" means to lead out of the right path and it has strong sexual connotations. She was leading them into immorality. The word "fornication" comes from the Greek word *pornia* and the English word pornography is derived from it. It refers to any sexual sin. The word literally means to prostitute one's body to the lusts of another. It can refer to sexual sin, or it can be used as a metaphor for idol worship. Regardless of what they were doing, the Lord calls it "the deep things of Satan" (v.24). The same teaching exists today where people who call themselves Christians live lives of open sin. The Lord told his people to separate from that kind of lifestyle:

### 2 Corinthians 6:16-17

16 What agreement has the temple of God with idols? For we are the temple of the living God; as God said,

"I will make my dwelling among them and walk among them,
    and I will be their God,
    and they shall be my people.
17 Therefore go out from their midst,
    and be separate from them, says the Lord,
and touch no unclean thing;
    then I will welcome you,

Christians have liberty but liberty is not a license to sin.

## Denounced by God

The Lord denounced her stubbornness (v.21). The Lord had given this woman and those who followed her time to turn from their sins but they refused to do so. God is a patient and loving. He gives lost sinners and wayward believers many opportunities to get right with him. When they refuse, they can expect judgment (Proverbs 29:1). The Lord as righteous judge declares sentence (v.22-23). Because of what she has done, she and all her followers will face God's wrath. The reference to "her children" in verse 23 could be taken literally or metaphorically. Young people suffer most when there is compromise and hypocrisy in the church. They see the inconsistency and they turn their backs on the church and God.

## Tolerance not Tolerated by God

Jesus confronted the tolerance of this church (v.20). He expressed displeasure with the church in Thyatira because they allowed this woman to be in a position of leadership. They tolerated the lies she was teaching as truth. God was deeply displeased that they would allow things of that nature to go on there. Some may have disliked it or disagreed with it but tolerated it.

When false doctrine is being preached in the church, those who know the truth have a duty to stand up and do something about it. To sit back and allow that kind of wickedness to go unchecked invites the anger and judgment of God. Many people like to be tolerant. Some churches pride themselves on their tolerance. Tolerance is not a virtue. Many people today seem to think that it is. It all depends on what one tolerates. In the same way as loyalty is not a virtue.

That too depends on what one is loyal to. God still expects his people to be different from the world around them. If a church behaves like Thyatira and compromises in order to appeal to the world it is turning its back on truth. When the door is opened to let the world come in, it should be no surprise if the Lord walks out.

## Confronting the Sinners

Therefore, Jesus confronted this church about its testimony. He told them that he would use them as an example to teach other churches what happens when truth is compromised. This is the language of a judge handing down a sentence. The church in Thyatira had been established to bring the Word of God to a pagan city. They had functioned well for a while but then they had abandoned the right path. They are going to pay a heavy price for their sin. When there is sin in the camp, the Lord will deal with it. He will remove his power and presence. *Ichabod* could be posted over its door.[85]

---

[85] Ichabod (Hebrew: אִי כָבוֹד inglorious) is named by the Books of Samuel as the brother of Ahitub. Ichabod is also identified by the Books of Samuel as having been the son of Phinehas, and as having been born on the day that the Ark was taken into Philistine captivity. His mother went into labor due to the shock of hearing that her husband and father-in-law had died and that the Ark had been captured. The identity and name of his mother is not given, and she is said to have died shortly after having given birth to him, and having named him. In the Book of 1 Samuel, his name is said to be a reference to the fact that the glory had departed from Israel, because of the loss of the Ark to the Philistines, and a lesser reference to the deaths of her father-in-law, Eli and her husband, Phinehas. She repeats the phrase, "The glory has departed from Israel, for the ark of God has been captured." This shows her piety in that the public and spiritual loss lay heavier upon her spirit than her personal or domestic calamity.

## Comforting the Saints

The Lord is very balanced in his comments to this wayward people. He *commended* them for their service, *confronted* them for their sin and now he *comforts* the saints in this church (vs. 24-29). Apparently, not everyone in Thyatira was living a compromised life. Even in that tolerant, compromising, sinful church there was a faithful remnant. The Lord had a few words of hope and comfort for them as they struggled to walk uprightly in an unholy generation and unholy congregation (vs. 24-25). Jesus told them that all he expected from them was that they stay the course. He wanted them to avoid being sucked into the vortex of evil that was swirling there in Thyatira. That is his will for all Churches in these confusing days as well. He wants Christians to stay the course for the glory of God.

## The Faithful will Rule

The Lord promised them that if they remain faithful to him, they would rule with him when he comes in his kingdom (vs.26-27). If the disciples of Jesus are to be a holy, godly people in these days, they might well be misunderstood, hated, and persecuted. The worldly, compromising churches might be the ones with larger congregations and prestige but, when the King comes, those who have served him faithfully now will reign with him then.[86]

Satan would love nothing better than to slither his way into a fellowship of believers and cause them to abandon the Lord's truth. The Christian church must be vigilant (1 Peter 5:8). There is a sacred body of doctrine, which must be

---

[86] Of course, I am not saying that large churches are compromised.

preserved. All Christians are custodians of the truth but Christian leaders have a particular responsibility as guardians of this corpus of divinity. Believers must watch out and work hard against the tactics of Satan. Sin comes into an assembly of believers when individual believers allow Satan a foothold in their lives. A foothold becomes a stronghold. Give Satan an inch and he will take a foot.

## Heresy Exposed

Therefore, the Lord came with joy to commend all who are faithful. Then he came in judgment to condemn those who were compromised. Heresy cannot be condoned and it cannot be ignored. The church must not become like the world to win the world. The church must not adopt an 'end justifies the means' approach. Attempts to adopt and incorporate worldliness into the church are often subtle. Sin must be called sin and it must never be condoned in the church. Doctrine is important. People are still twisting the truth. The history of the church shows that heresy is a continuing problem. The Lord will punish those who are guilty of distorting the truth. He will *recognize* and *reward* the faithful. Those who remain faithful to the truth will be blessed.

# A Message to the Church in Sardis

# Autopsy of a Dead Church

These letters from Jesus to the seven churches in Asia Minor were written to real churches in the first century but they speak to churches in every age and location. These words from Jesus tell us what he expects from a church. Therefore, there is a message here for today. This is the post-mortem of a dead church. People in this world are spiritually thirsty and they need the living water of life. People in this world are spiritually hungry and they need the bread of life. Many people go to so-called churches expecting to quench their thirst with the water of life and to satisfy their hunger with the bread of life. These poor souls enter buildings where they hope to find God but all they find is dead religion and lifeless rituals. Many people, desperate for help and hope, enter these dead-houses. They call themselves churches but they are museums to tradition. They may have cathedrals, architectural grandeur, wealth, robes, rituals and rites but no life.[87] Sardis was a church that had a reputation for being alive but it was dead. The church in Sardis had taken on the character of the city of Sardis.

## Background

A little background on the city will help us understand the condition of this church. Sardis was the capital city of Lydia. It was founded about 1,200 BC. The original city sat on the top of a 1,500-foot high plateau. There was one narrow road leading into the city. The other sides of the

---

[87] These features in themselves do not necessarily indicate deadness. It is possible to have cathedrals, architectural grandeur, wealth, robes, rituals and rites and also have vibrant life in a church, as many will attest.

plateau were just steep cliffs. This made the city very safe and nearly impenetrable by invading armies.

Sardis was the home of Aesop the author of so many fables. Gold and silver coins were first minted there. The city of Sardis was famous for the industries that operated there. Carpet, wool and dyed cloth were their primary products. It is said that the art of dyeing was invented at Sardis. At one time, Sardis had been one of the greatest cities in the world. It reached its zenith under King Croesus. King Croesus and Sardis were famed around the world for their wealth. In that part of the world, it is still common to hear the phrase, 'as wealthy as Croesus'.

### Complacency

While Sardis reached its zenith under Croesus, it also fell under his reign. He and the people of the city became complacent in their wealth, their power and their city's apparent invincibility.

The region where Sardis was located came under attack by Cyrus the Persian King. Croesus and his people retreated to their city, believing they were safe. One night, one of the Persian soldiers saw a Sardis soldier drop his helmet over the wall of the city. He watched as that soldier followed a hidden path down the side of the mountain to retrieve his helmet. When nightfall came, Cyrus and his troops followed the hidden path up the side of the mountain. They entered the city while the guards slept and conquered Sardis.

Sardis regained some of its former wealth under the reign of Alexander the Great. But it was invaded and defeated by Antiochus the Great, who also entered the city at night while the guards slept. When the Romans came, Sardis was still a wealthy, powerful city, but it was just a shell of its former self. Therefore, by John's day, Sardis was just a shadow of what it had been. The people had grown lazy, immoral and complacent. Sardis was dying through apathy and indifference. The city was proud of its past. It was proud of its reputation. However, its reputation was all it had left. It was a dying city. It is to this church that had become lazy, apathetic and complacent that Jesus spoke.

## The Great Physician

The Great Physician performs an autopsy on this dead church. Here is his autopsy report. The seven Spirits of God are mentioned four times in the book of Revelation (Revelation 1:4; 3:1; 4:5; 5:6). The "Sevenfold Ministry of the Spirit" interpretation holds that the seven Spirits refer to the book of Isaiah (cf. Isaiah 11:2) which speaks of the Spirit of the Lord, of wisdom, of understanding, of counsel, of might, of knowledge, and the fear of the Lord. This was a reminder to the churches that Christians are to operate, not under the power of human skill, leadership and organization but under the awesome power of the Holy Spirit.

When the church walks in the power of the flesh it will surely fail. However, when a church walks in the power of the Spirit, there will be success. There will be glory, power and life instead of deadness and ineffectiveness. Jesus appeared as one who has everything the church needs to succeed. His Spirit has all the power the church needs. His Word has all the direction his churches need. That is a message the church needs today. Many are trying every method under the sun to reach sinners, and to do the work of the church. This is commendable.[88] But, all the power needed is found in the fullness of the Holy Ghost and in the

---

[88] This is good if it does not involve compromising the integrity of the message of the gospel.

Word of God. What is needed is not a new method but a new desire to seek the fullness of the Holy Spirit and do everything according to the teachings of the Word of God.

Jesus told them, "I know your works". He discerns all things. The psalmist puts this eloquently:

**Psalm 139:1-4**

1 O Lord, you have searched me and known me!
2 You know when I sit down and when I rise up;
    you discern my thoughts from afar.
3 You search out my path and my lying down
    and are acquainted with all my ways.
4 Even before a word is on my tongue,
    behold, O Lord, you know it altogether.

He knows the motives of the human heart. Apparently, the works of the church in Sardis gave them the appearance of life. They had the reputation of a church that was alive. The outward appearance looked good. However, things were not as they seemed. The Great Physician placed his finger on the pulse of this church and pronounced them dead. They were not just ill but deceased. No matter what others thought, Jesus knew the truth.

### Dictionary Definition

The dictionary definition of the word 'dead' is interesting. At the risk of this sounding like the Monty Python sketch about the dead parrot, which incorporates a host of synonyms like a thesaurus into a very funny dialogue, this may be offered, dead means having passed from the living state to being no longer alive. It can also mean never having been alive. It means having none of the characteristics of a living thing or unable to support life (like a dead planet). It means having lost normal sensitivity to touch or pain, from the effects of cold, disease, or anesthesia (e.g. "my fingers have gone completely dead"). Another definition is: unable or unwilling to respond to, understand, or appreciate something (e.g. "she seemed completely dead to her surroundings"). It means showing no indication of feeling or vitality. The application is obvious. Pardon the pun, this is a grave matter. Jesus told them that even though everyone thought they were alive, they were, in fact, dead.

## Looks can be Deceiving

Therefore, the church at Sardis was dead. What does this mean? There was activity, but it was not spiritual in nature. There was busyness, but they were bringing nothing eternal to pass. They were operating in the energy of the flesh and not the power of the Spirit of God.

Looks can be deceiving. Picked flowers have all the appearance of life. They are beautiful, colorful, and fragrant but they are dead. They have been severed from the roots that gave them life. Soon their colors will fade, their blooms wilt and their leaves turn brown and they will be thrown away. They look alive, but they are dead. They once had life but now they do not.[89] Synthetic flowers look like the real thing but they are not. Whereas real flowers that have been cut once had life synthetic flowers never had life. The church is an organism, a living, dynamic entity. It is to be authentic not synthetic. The same can be said about animals on display in a museum. They look very life-like. They are placed in natural habitats, but they are dead. Our world is filled with similar fakes, such as wax fruit.

---

[89] This does not mean that they were once saved but now they have lost their salvation. It could mean that they never had any real spiritual life in the first place or that they have lost their authentic, dynamic living faith.

Astronomers tell us that it takes thirty-three years for the light from the Polar Star to reach the earth. For all we know the Polar Star might have burned out twenty years ago and we would not know it for another thirteen years. It looks like it is still there, but it may not be. It could be a dead star.

## Application

Many churches have the appearance of life, but the Great Physician has his finger on their pulse and he knows they are dead. The crucial question for each local congregation is how is its pulse? Is it strong and steady? Or, is it weak and failing? Each individual Christian ought to ask if his heart throbs with love for Jesus?

## Symptoms of Critical Illness

Here are some of the signs that a church is dying. A dying church rests on its past accomplishments and is satisfied with its present state. A dying church is more concerned with rituals and traditions than it is about spirituality. It is more interested in material growth than it is with spiritual growth. It is more interested in pleasing men than pleasing God is. A dying church clings more tightly to its creeds and confessions that it does to the Word of God. A dying church is one that loses its conviction that the Bible is the Word of God.

### Indicators of health

Here are the signs of life in a church. Growth is an obvious sign of life. All living things are characterized by growth. This does not necessarily mean numerical growth. There is a discernible pattern to the process of growth in a church. First, growth takes place in the hearts and minds of individual members of a church. They become more mature in understanding and in love. A growing together in unity of purpose follows this. The third and final stage in this process of growth may or may not be numerical growth.

Harmony, therefore, is a very healthy sign in a church. When a physical body develops problems, it is because there is disharmony in the body. Cancer is an example of this. The cancer infects some of the cells and they attack other cells in the body. If this is left unchecked, the result will be disintegration and death for that body. The same is true in the church. When a church is alive and well, there will be unity and harmony in the fellowship.

### Emotion and Motion

Another mark of life in the physical realm is emotion. Because people are alive they can laugh, cry, feel pain, and joy. Healthy people have emotions and this demonstrates the fact that they are alive. When a physical body dies, one of the clearest indications is the total lack of emotion.

Again, the same is true in the church. A living church is an emotional church. There will be times when the congregation will laugh together and there will be times when they weep together. In other words, where there is life, there is emotion.

Another sign of life is motion. Physical bodies are organisms in motion. One sure sign of death is the absence of motion. Therefore, it is within the church. When there is life in a church, there will be motion. This means that the church will be active in the world doing the work of the Lord.

### From Pronouncement to Prescription

Therefore, that is the Great Physician's pronouncement, which is followed by his prescription (vs. 2-3). Lack of motion is not a sure sign of death. A person could be asleep or in a coma. The physician will not pronounce death on such a body or write a death certificate. The church in Sardis

126

was not just asleep. They were dead. Only the power of God can revive such a corpse. At the word of Jesus, Lazarus was raised from the dead. At Christ's command, Jairus' daughter was raised from the dead. Jesus spoke and the widow of Nain's son was raised from the dead.

### Wake-up Call

The church in Sardis is commanded to wake up. A church can have a glorious past but it should not allow its past success to lull it into a state of complacency and spiritual slumber. Jesus calls on this church to wake up and realize that the victories of yesterday are not sufficient for this day.

The people in Sardis would have understood exactly what Jesus was talking about. As mentioned earlier, Sardis was located on the top of a mountain. It had one entrance on the southern side, which was the only way one could get into the city. Therefore, all that Sardis had to do was to put sentries at that one place to watch the city. However, on two occasions in their history their enemies had invaded them. Once because they had felt secure, believing that the hill was impregnable and on another occasion because the sentry went to sleep on the job. In 549 B.C., the soldiers of Cyrus scaled the parapet. Then again, in 218 B.C. Antiochus the Great captured Sardis because the sentries were careless.

### Loss of Vision and Vitality

This happens far too often in churches. A church will struggle in its beginning and the core group who founded that church will have to work, pray, witness, give and yield to God to see the church stay alive. Over time, more people come in and more money comes in. Buildings are built and good services are enjoyed. Then the church begins to lose the vision and vitality that made them so strong in their early years. They become content to sit back and enjoy the fruits of their labors. It is okay to look back to the past with pride but not to dwell there. The Christian vision ought to be for today and for tomorrow.

### Feeding the Fire

A fire must be fed if it is to stay alive. I remember that on one occasion when I was teaching theology on leadership training programs in Serbia I was staying in a small-prefabricated chalet. It was freezing cold in Nis (the second largest city in Serbia, after Belgrade). There was thick snow on the ground and it was twenty degrees below zero. The walls of the chalet were not insulated but there was a wood-burning stove in the room and this was a blessing. The person in charge of my accommodation lit the fire on the evening of my first night there and soon the room was quite cozy. He left me with a supply of firewood. I went to bed and quickly fell fast asleep. However, I woke in the middle of the night and the room was freezing. I could see my breath in the form of a freezing fog and the moisture on the insides of the windows had frozen to ice. The fire had gone out. I had a supply of firewood but no means of igniting a fire. I tried to revive the dying embers by blowing on them but alas, my attempts were in vain. After several failed attempts to light the fire, I realized the futility of my efforts and decided to put on several layers of clothes and pull the blanket over my head until somebody arrived to rescue me in the morning. One could die in such sub-zero temperatures. The fire needed to be fed in order to keep it alive and the consequences of not doing that could have been fatal.

This is true of the spiritual life. We must feed the spiritual fire with the fuel it needs: prayer and reading the Scriptures. If these matters are not attended to, the outcome can be disastrous. Believers must fight the tendency to become smug and complacent and they must give their souls enough fuel to keep their passion for Jesus alive and burning hot.

### Work

The church in Sardis was told to work. The Lord said, "strengthen what remains". They were asked to clear away the dead ash and put fresh kindling in place. Then the Lord would provide the spark and blow the flame into fire. They were called to respond appropriately.

They were to remember what they had received and heard. This is a sacred duty, to preserve and promote the truth intact. They were to remember their redemption and every vital encounter with the Lord. They were to remember the days when they served the Lord out of glad hearts and wanted more than anything to do his will. They were not to be complacent about it and say they had done their bit, and assume they can take it easy now.

### Repentance, Restoration and Revival

They are confronted concerning their sin. When there is sin in the life of an individual, there must be repentance before there can be restoration and revival. The same is true for a church. They were told to be watchful because the Lord would come as a thief. As bad as things were in Sardis, there were some there who were saved and seeking to serve the Lord. They were given the Lord's promise that they would walk with the Lord in white. They have lived out the truth in this world.

### Purity, Victory and Festivity

White clothing was worn in Roman times during festivals and times of celebration. It was a symbol of purity, victory and festivity. What a promise to the faithful members of that church. Jesus said that they are standing faithful. You have not defiled your garments with the deadness that exists all around you. You are saved and you are serving. One day, you will walk with me in heaven. It will be a time of victory, festivity and purity. Jesus said that those who repent will "be clothed in white robes". They will be made pure and victorious.

The Lord said, "The one who conquers will be clothed thus in white garments, and I will never blot his name out of the book of life. I will confess his name before my Father and before his angels" (3:5). What did Jesus mean when he said, "I will never blot his name out of the book of life"? These wonderful words addressed to believers are sometimes misunderstood. People who try to say that Christians can lose their salvation often use them.[90] This is not the meaning of Christ's words. Perhaps the reason is that some Christians do not understand what is meant by "The one who conquers" or the "overcomer". Who is an overcomer? This question is clearly answered,

### 1 John 5:4-5

**4** For everyone who has been born of God overcomes the world. And this is the victory that has overcome the world— our faith. **5** Who is it that overcomes the world except the one who believes that Jesus is the Son of God?

Therefore, an overcomer is clearly a believer in the Lord Jesus Christ. A believer becomes an overcomer not on the basis of good deeds but on the basis of the finished work of Jesus Christ on the cross at Calvary. So the words of Jesus

---

[90] The reader is encouraged by Christian publishing House to consider the article, Salvation - Can We Lose It?

http://www.christianpublishers.org/salvation-can-you-lose-it

here are addressed to those that are born of God, those who have trusted Jesus Christ as their Savior. The overcomer does not *purchase* his salvation by perseverance rather he *proves* his salvation by perseverance in the faith.

### First Promise

The first promise to the believer in Revelation 3:5 says, "The one who conquers will be clothed thus in white garments." This is a picture of the righteousness of God, which is required for salvation. The Lord has taken the inadequate piety of the believer (rags) and clothed them in robes of righteousness: 'But we are all as an unclean thing and all our righteousnesses are as filthy rags...' (Isaiah 64:6). Earlier in the book of Isaiah these wonderful words may be found, 'I will greatly rejoice in the LORD; my soul shall exult in my God, for he has clothed me with the garments of salvation; he has covered me with the robe of righteousness' (Isaiah 61:10). Therefore, the promise is that every believer (overcomer) shall be clothed in white robes. This speaks of the righteousness of God: 'For our sake he made him to be sin who knew no sin, so that in him we might become the righteousness of God.'—2 Corinthians 5:21.

### Second Promise

The second promise to the believer in Revelation 3:5 says, "I will never blot his name out of the book of life". This shows how the Lord knows who belongs to him. It teaches that he is ever mindful of them and they are secure in him. Those whose names are written in the book of life will never have their names erased or deleted.

At the final judgment, unbelievers are cast into the lake of fire[91] and their names will not be found in the book of life. (Rev. 20:10-15). A most interesting Scripture on this point is found in Exodus 32. The children of Israel had greatly sinned against the Lord in making gods of gold to worship. Moses interceded on behalf of the people:

## Exodus 32:31-33

[31] So Moses returned to the Lord and said, "Alas, this people has sinned a great sin. They have made for themselves gods of gold. [32] But now, if you will forgive their sin—but if not, please blot me out of your book that you have written." [33] But the Lord said to Moses, "Whoever has sinned against me, I will blot out of my book.

Many people assume that Moses is talking about the book of life. If Moses was talking about the book of life, and saying that he would be willing to die and be lost forever for his people's sake; then he, like the apostle Paul, would just be using a figure of speech to show how much they longed to see their people saved. The apostle Paul said:

## Romans 9:1-4

[1] I am speaking the truth in Christ—I am not lying; my conscience bears me witness in the Holy Spirit—[2] that I have great sorrow and unceasing anguish in my heart. [3] For I could wish that I myself were accursed and cut off from Christ for the sake of my brothers, my kinsmen according to the flesh. [4] They are Israelites, and to them belong the

---

[91] Christian Publishing House would encourage readers to read the articles, Hellfire - Eternal Torment? And Hellfire - Is It Just?

http://www.christianpublishers.org/hellfire-eternal-torment

http://www.christianpublishers.org/hellfire-is-it-just

adoption, the glory, the covenants, the giving of the law, the worship, and the promises.

Sometimes people say, "I'd give my right arm to have a car like that". That is just a figure of speech. Even if they would give their right arm, it would not help them get the car. Even so, if Moses and Paul could have somehow given up their own salvation, it would have done no good for their people, because both Moses and Paul were sinners, and they could not save anyone. Only the unblemished Lamb of God could atone for sin.

When the Lord replied to Moses, "Whoever has sinned against me, I will blot out of my book" he was not talking about the "book of life" but about the "book of the living" containing the names of those who are presently alive upon earth. Psalm 69:26-28 says, "Let them be blotted out of the book of the living; let them not be enrolled among the righteous." God has a book in which is written the name of every person alive upon earth. When that person dies, his/her name is blotted out of that book.

The Bible is clear that sometimes God does take people out of the book of the living because of sin (that is, their sin is of such nature that God requires their lives for it. (1 Jn. 5:16-17). To say that God blots names out of the book of life would be to contradict the clear teaching of Scripture. The names of those people who do not receive the Lord Jesus Christ were never registered in the book of life.

### Liberty not License

A lifestyle of habitual sin is an indication that no true spiritual life exists. Revelation 3:5 teaches that those who believe on the Lord Jesus Christ will *not* have their names blotted out. The believer will be clothed with the righteousness of God, and his name will never be blotted out of the book of life. It is recorded in the Gospel of John that Jesus said: "All that the Father gives me will come to me, and whoever comes to me I will never cast out." (Jn 6:37) Later on, he said, "My sheep hear my voice, and I know them, and they follow me. I give them eternal life, and they will never perish, and no one will snatch them out of my hand." (Jn. 10:27-28) If the believer's eternal salvation depended on the believer then one could lose it but because it is based on the perfect and completed work of Christ, the believer's eternal destiny is secure.[92] The Christian can rest in his substitutionary atonement. Those who truly belong to Jesus will not abuse the privilege of such grace. The believer enjoys liberty in Christ but this is not a license to indulge in sinfulness. The believer will walk in the light but occasionally he will stumble in the darkness and at such times, the penitent saint who has sinned can find forgiveness.—1 John 1:8-9.

### Third Promise

The third promise to the believer in Revelation 3:5 is expressed in these words of Christ, "I will confess his name before my Father, and before his angels." One day Jesus will say about those who demonstrated the reality of their faith by being faithful to him: "This is one of mine! He was not ashamed of me and I am not ashamed of him!" However, the majority in the church in Sardis was not just cold and out of God's will. They were lost, dead sinners in need of salvation.[93] There are many churches like this. Most of the congregations in such churches are not Christians. They may

---

[92] Readers, for additional information, please read, Salvation - Can We Lose It?

http://www.christianpublishers.org/salvation-can-you-lose-it

[93] In this sense, they would not be members of the church but they would be people who attended the gatherings of Christians.

be Christian in name and even pious in their lifestyles but such nominal 'Christianity' is not real Christianity. Churches in that shape do not need revival they need a resurrection.

There is always the danger that any church can die. That is to say it, as a corporate community of believers, can cease to exist. It is not that believers in such churches lose their salvation, rather that the light of their temporal witness is extinguished.

I have never tried and do not intend ever to conduct such an experiment. I believe that one could put a frog in a kettle of cold water and switch it on, and although the water would get gradually hotter until it eventually boils, the frog will not jump out. Why? I can only assume that the frog becomes acclimatized to the gradual increase in temperature and eventually either falls asleep or becomes paralyzed. I suspect it enjoys the warm water up to a point and then becomes weakened by it. Some people in churches are like that frog. They become gradually become accustomed to conditions that will eventually overpower them and bring about spiritual deadness.

If the Great Physician were to put his finger on the pulse of every member of the church what would his touch reveal about us?

# A Message to the Church in Philadelphia

# Christt the Concierge

**P**hiladelphia was the youngest and smallest of all the cities addressed in these letters. The city was located in a narrow pass between two mountain ranges. It stood as a literal doorway between Asia Minor and Asia. Enemy armies passing through the narrow pass could be delayed by a small force at Philadelphia. The city was named for King Attalus II, the king of Pergamum. He was renowned for his love of his brother Eumenes, and he came to be called 'Philadelphos'. The word means 'brotherly love'.

Philadelphia was built on a geological fault and plagued by frequent earthquakes and tremors. The citizens were often forced to flee the city to avoid being injured or killed by falling buildings.

Philadelphia had numerous temples dedicated to various gods and goddesses. It was the last of the seven cities to lose its Christian testimony. There was a thriving Christian community there as late as 1,000 A.D., when the Muslim armies of the Middle East captured the city.

## The Holy One

Here the doorkeeper speaks. Jesus identified himself in two powerful ways. First, Jesus identified himself as "the holy one." The word "holy" asserts that Jesus is sinless and pure. That is the Bible's testimony about Jesus: 'He committed no sin, neither was deceit found in his mouth.'—1 Peter 2:22.

That is also hell's testimony about Jesus. The Gospel of Mark records an incident when a man with an unclean spirit addressed Jesus. Before Jesus performed a miraculous healing in this man's life the man said, "What have you to do with us, Jesus of Nazareth? Have you come to destroy us? I know who you are---the Holy One of God."—Mark 1:24.

This is also heaven's testimony concerning Christ. When the birth of Jesus was foretold to Mary: 'And the angel answered her, "The Holy Spirit will come upon you, and the power of the Most High will overshadow you; therefore the child to be born will be called holy---the Son of God.'—Luke 1:35.

This was also Jesus' testimony about himself when he asked the rhetorical question, "Which one of you convicts me of sin?" (Jn. 8:46). The clear implication is that Jesus is proclaiming his sinlessness.

Here in the book of Revelation Jesus is speaking to the church in Philadelphia. It is a church that is striving to be holy in the midst of a sinful world. The Lord has the power to help the Christian live the holy lives he desires them to live.

### The True One

Second, Jesus identifies himself as "the true one". These early believers were surrounded daily by that which was false. False gods and false worship abounded in that day. Jesus came to them declaring that he was to be regarded as "true". Jesus said to Pilate, "For this purpose I was born and for this purpose I have come into the world---to bear witness to the truth. Everyone who is of the truth listens to my voice." (Jn. 18:37) Pilate asked derisively "What is truth?"—John 18:38.

Jesus said, "I am the way, and the truth, and the life. No one comes to the Father except through me" (Jn. 14:6). Jesus is called "faithful and true" (Rev. 3:14; 19:11). This is not just his *name* it is also his *nature*. The Lord is holy and true. There is no sin and there is no deception in Christ. Jesus is good and dependable and he invites people into relationship.

## Doors

There are spiritual doors in life. Some doors are open and others are closed. The Lord is the doorkeeper. The church in Philadelphia was weak in power but strong in the Lord. A door can be either an entrance or a barrier. It represents either access or denial, depending on whether it is open or closed.[94] A door represents a transition from one place to another. One can be inside or outside. Doors feature frequently in Scripture in a literal or figurative way. In this passage, the "open door" is symbolic and speaks of opportunity.

The apostle Paul once wrote these words: 'But I will stay in Ephesus until Pentecost, for a wide door for effective work has opened to me' (1 Cor. 16:8-9). Jesus said, "Ask, and it will be given to you; seek, and you will find; knock, and it will be opened to you. For everyone who asks receives, and the one who seeks finds, and to the one who knocks it will be opened." (Matt. 7:7-8) These words of Jesus recorded in Matthew's Gospel speak of answered prayer as the opening of a door. They speak of blessing.

The open and shut doors of life have the ability to change the course of life. In Acts 12:1-17, Simon Peter was in prison and scheduled to die the next morning. God sent and angel and opened the doors of liberty for him. The doors of the prison opened, the gates of the city opened, but when he arrived at the house where the church was praying for his release, Peter found the door shut! These doors changed Peter's life.

---

[94] A door can also be a point of egress and sometimes it is necessary to leave an unhealthy church via the doors the Lord provides.

Paul experienced two closed doors that led him to God's open door of ministry,

### Acts 16:6-10

⁶ And they went through the region of Phrygia and Galatia, having been forbidden by the Holy Spirit to speak the word in Asia. ⁷ And when they had come up to Mysia, they attempted to go into Bithynia, but the Spirit of Jesus did not allow them. ⁸ So, passing by Mysia, they went down to Troas. ⁹ And a vision appeared to Paul in the night: a man of Macedonia was standing there, urging him and saying, "Come over to Macedonia and help us." ¹⁰ And when Paul had seen the vision, immediately we sought to go on into Macedonia, concluding that God had called us to preach the gospel to them.

These doors changed, not only the direction of Paul's life, but also the course of world history.

An open door is generally a good thing. It is a cause of rejoicing when the door of opportunity is opened. When God opens a door, the believer should step through that door, by faith, without hesitation, because God is doing something special in such person's life.

A closed door, by contrast, brings disappointment. Often the followers of Jesus want to do what they want rather than what God wants and do not like to hear God say "No". The closed doors of life are just as meaningful as the open doors. In the spiritual journey, the Lord's disciples will encounter open doors and closed doors. When God closes a door, the Christian should walk away from it. The temptation is to try to force it, but this must be resisted. The believer should pay close attention to open and closed doors for ministry. It is wise to step through every door he opens and stay away from those he closes.

## Christ as Concierge

Christ is the head of the church assuming the lowly position of concierge. He is the doorkeeper who opens and closes doors as it pleases him. He holds the keys and he determines which doors are opened and which remain closed. The Lord is intimately involved in the lives of his people, "For I know the plans I have for you, declares the LORD, plans for welfare and not for evil, to give you a future and a hope." (Jer. 29:11) These comforting words were spoken to the Lord's people at a time when all hopeless. Every open door is an expression of his love and of his activity in the lives of his people. So is every closed door. Whatever kind of doors one faces in life the children of God should know that the Lord is the one who opens and shuts the doors of life. The Christian must step through them or walk away from them as appropriate.

## Access to the Treasures of the Kingdom

The Lord did not reprimand the church in Philadelphia. Everything that Jesus said to them was positive. Here is a model church. Jesus is described as holding the "key of David". This is a reference to a prophecy in Isaiah 22:20-22 concerning a faithful man named Eliakim, the steward of King Hezekiah. He was given the "key of David." This referred to the fact that Eliakim had access to all the riches that belonged to the king:

### Isaiah 22:20-22

20 In that day I will call my servant Eliakim the son of Hilkiah, 21 and I will clothe him with your robe, and will bind your sash on him, and will commit your authority to his hand. And he shall be a father to the inhabitants of Jerusalem and to the house of Judah. 22 And I will place on his

shoulder the key of the house of David. He shall open, and none shall shut; and he shall shut, and none shall open.

This Old Testament passage speaks *literally* of Eliakim and *figuratively* of the Lord Jesus Christ. He is the faithful administrator of the riches of the kingdom of his heavenly Father.

In these words from Isaiah, one must recognize the *Sensus Plenior* of Scripture.[95] The term *Sensus Plenior* (fuller sense) helps the student of Scripture to understand that Old Testament history and prophecy might have a deeper and more far-reaching meaning, which may or may not have been discerned by the original human author. The fuller meaning is made clear by the subsequent revelation of the Holy Spirit in the New Testament. As one author put it:

> ...the author does not intentionally convey the sensus plenior to his hearers. But at a later date, in the light of further revelation, the fuller meaning becomes clear to readers under the influence of the Spirit who inspired the original author.[96]

The *sensus plenior* helps the reader of God's Word to see the deeper theological purpose behind certain events and persons within biblical history. These are not arbitrary meanings discovered by a creative interpreter. They are not just chosen or determined at random. They are not based solely on personal wishes, feelings, or perceptions. As the

---

[95] Christian Publishing House Note: Dear Reader, for a more detailed look into the important subject of a New Testament writers use of the Old Testament, please read the article, New Testament Writers Use of the Old Testament

http://www.christianpublishers.org/nt-writers-use-of-the-ot

[96] William LaSor, 'Interpretation of Prophecy', *Hermeneutics*, ed. Bernard Ramm, (Baker Grand Rapids, Michigan: 1987, p.108).

theologian, Louis Berkhof has stated, 'The real meaning of Scripture does not always lie on the surface.'[97]

This passage in Revelation reminds the reader that Jesus has the power to meet the needs of his church. Since he has the keys, he is has the power to open and close doors as he sees fit. All the doors of God are a blessing. There are times when he opens wide the doors and there is no doubt about his will. There are other times when doors are slammed shut and when that happens, it can be confusing and disappointing. When the Lord closes a door in the life of a believer, he is going to lead that person in another direction where he has opened a door. It takes grace to accept the closed doors as well as the open doors.

These people are described as having little strength. While the church of Philadelphia was weak from a human point of view, they were faithful. The words of the apostle Paul seem particularly apt: 'For when I am weak, then I am strong' (2 Cor. 12:10). Weakness forces the child of God into a place of greater dependence upon the Lord and in this the Lord is glorified.

### Three Traits

This church had three traits that made them strong in the midst of their weakness. First, they kept the Word of God. This church honored the Word of God. They gave it a high place in their church and in their lives. When the Bible spoke, they listened and obeyed. The Bible is under attack in the present day and many have departed from its teachings. However, for a church to be strong in the Lord, the Bible

---

[97] Louis Berkhof, *Principles of Biblical Interpretation*, (Grand Rapids, Michigan: Baker, 1950 p.59).

must be that church's mandate. A people who want to be blessed should honor the Word of God.

Second, they had not denied the Lord's name. They were not ashamed to be identified with the name of Jesus. They were not ashamed to exalt him and allow him to be the focus of their worship and their lives. If Jesus is the center of the church's work and worship then the church will be blessed.

Third, they are commended for their "patient endurance". Patience is the ability to endure waiting, delay, or provocation without becoming annoyed or upset, or to persevere calmly when faced with difficulties. In the spiritual life one frequently has to wait. There are delays and interruptions. Things do not always go according to plan. The spiritual challenge is to endure such delays and frustrations with a calm dignity, which demonstrates the serenity that the child of God possesses in Christ. Patience is about maintaining a calm spirit that is resting in the sovereign will of God and persevering when faced with difficulties. This church is commended for this virtue. It is a fruit of the Spirit. It is evidence of his indwelling and controlling influence.

### Opposition and Opportunities

The word endurance speaks of the ability to bear prolonged pain or hardship. The power to do that comes from the Lord. The Lord presents the believer with opportunities for worship, work and witness. However, there will also be opposition. The church in Philadelphia had enemies. They were Jewish people who refused to receive Jesus as the Messiah. These Jews opposed the work of the early Christians and persecuted them. Of course, the real enemy was not Judaism but Satan:

144

### Ephesians 6:12

[12] For we do not wrestle against flesh and blood, but against the rulers, against the authorities, against the cosmic powers over this present darkness, against the spiritual forces of evil in the heavenly places.

However, the Lord promised that they would be vindicated and their enemies would be humiliated. The believer must stay true to the Word and uphold the name of Jesus, in spite of opposition from family or the community. The local church today in many parts of the world experiences opposition but there are also many opportunities.

### Obligations

Furthermore, the church today has obligations. The Philadelphian believers were counseled to hold onto the things they had: that is God's Word and to honor the Lord's name. The church today should take a good inventory of where it is in relation to such counsel. Every local body of believers needs to be sure that they continue in these things. The Lord told them to carry on. Sometimes a believer might feel like giving up but the Lord says keep going! There will be a day when those who are faithful and obedient will be rewarded. The Christian must continue walking with the Lord, worshipping the Lord and witnessing for the Lord.

### Pillars in a New Community

The ancient city of Philadelphia was filled with many pagan temples. It was the practice in Philadelphia for citizens who served the city to be honored by having a pillar with their name engraved on it placed in one of the pagan temples.

Jesus told his people that they would be honored by being made a pillar in his eternal temple. This speaks of security in Christ. If the believer wants to be a pillar in the church, he needs to be faithful to God's Word and to the Lord's name.

As already noted Philadelphia was built on a geological fault, and as a result, there were earthquakes that destroyed the city. When this happened, the pagan temples fell and had to be rebuilt. In 17 BC, an earthquake destroyed Philadelphia and many of the people did not return to the city. They stayed in the countryside. No such problems will affect the temple of God. There is strength, stability and security in the Lord.

## The Praises of Christ

Of our Lord's seven letters to the churches in Asia Minor, only two did not receive any sort of correction or rebuke, Smyrna (2:8-11) and Philadelphia (3:7-13). The other five letters all contain words of complaint and correction, but this church receives nothing but praise from the Lord Jesus Christ. This was a church that brought glory to God.

## The Key-Holder

Jesus has the key of David. What are keys for? People usually have car keys, house keys, and perhaps keys to their places of work. The idea of keys conveys two thoughts: access and authority. The person who has the keys can allow or deny admittance. Jesus is described here as the key man. He holds the keys of salvation. He alone can unlock and lock heaven, thereby granting or denying access. He alone can unlock and lock hell. He holds the keys of service. Jesus alone unlocks the doors of ministry. When he opens a door of service the believer should go through it. When he closes a door of service, the believer should accept it and move on.

No amount of pleading, pushing or pounding will open that door.

### Standards

Jesus knew that this church had little power. This possibly means that they were a small church with limited resources and few workers. This was a church that was walking in obedience to the Word of God. Scripture was their standard of faith and they refused to deviate from it.

Statements of faith are being diluted all the time so that certain unpalatable doctrines are omitted or deemphasized. The Lord will bless a church that is faithful to the Word of God. Obedience to Scripture is proof of love for God. Jesus said, "If you love me, you will keep my commandments" (Jn 14:15). Those who love him hold his Word in high regard and that honors him and he, in turn, honors that.

The Philadelphian believers had not denied the name of Jesus. They honored the Lord's name and this is the kind of church every church ought to strive to be. They are promised that they will stand as pillars in the temple of God in heaven. Of all the pagan temples that stood in Philadelphia, with all their thousands of pillars, none is still standing today. The honor of men is fleeting, but the honor the Lord bestows and promises in heaven is eternal. Which is preferable: temporary recognition here on earth or eternal recognition in heaven?

### A Place of Safety

Verse 12 speaks of "The one who conquers". Jesus says of such a person: "I will make him a pillar in the temple of my God. Never shall he go out of it." Philadelphia was built near an active volcano. When that mountain began to rumble, the citizens of the city were forced to flee. It was a very unsafe place to live. Jesus reminded them that they were headed to a place of safety in heaven.

Those who have the door of heaven opened to them find a place of eternal security. They will be identified as the people of God forever. They will have his name upon them. The apostle Paul reminded the Philippians (who were proud of their Roman citizenship) that their 'citizenship is in heaven' (Phil. 3:20). This is something believers today should note.

## Dependable, Dedicated, Devoted

The Philadelphian church was dependable, dedicated and devoted. Jesus had no complaint against this church. Instead, he had words of praise and words of promise. It is a model church and its testimony pleases the Lord. As already noted, this church did not have great power. That might mean that they were small in number and not very influential. Though they were weak in some ways, they were pure and strong in doctrine. They kept his Word. That means preserving it and promoting it. Effectively this means hearing and heeding it, loving it, living it, and sharing it. The Christian must not deny his name. To deny the name of the Lord means minimizing Jesus (his unique and universal claims) to draw a crowd. He must be the centerpiece of worship. The Christian must love the book and live the book. The followers of Jesus must love Jesus and lift Jesus.

## Synagogue of Satan

The phrase "synagogue of Satan" probably refers to the local Jews who were persecuting them. This church was suffering at the hands of people who claimed to love God, but they were lying. Jesus told them that he was aware of their mistreatment. He wanted them to know that a day was coming when those who opposed them would experience total defeat.

Biblical churches will be ridiculed, maligned and persecuted. Jesus said, "For everyone who does wicked things hates the light and does not come to the light, lest his works should be exposed" (Jn. 3:20). Jesus is coming and his people need to be ready to meet him. That means living as if he might come at any minute and involves working as if the time is short.

### Special Delivery

The people in the church of Philadelphia had no security in the city where they lived. But, they had eternal security in their relationship with Jesus Christ and in his kingdom. Jesus purchased the church with his precious blood and he has registered each saint for special delivery to his or her new home in glory. Verse 12 says, "I will write on him the name of my God, and the name of the city of my God, the new Jerusalem, which comes down from my God out of heaven, and my own new name." Elsewhere in the New Testament, the words of Jesus are recorded, "I give them eternal life, and they will never perish, and no one will snatch them out of my hand" (Jn. 10:28). Hallelujah!

# A Message to the Church in Laodicea

# A Lukewarm Church

The Lord was pleased with two of the seven churches (Smyrna and Philadelphia). The other five had serious problems. In order to understand the Lord's words to this church a little background on the city of Laodicea will help. This city was founded by Antiochus II sometime before 253 BC. It was named after his wife Laodice.

The city was located on a high plateau and was very secure from enemy attack. The one defensive problem in Laodicea was the fact that there was no ready source of water in the city. Water had to be piped in through aqueducts. Water from the hot springs in Hierapolis, six miles to the north, was brought into the city. Water was also piped in from Colossae, which was located ten miles to the east. This fact will be important in coming to an understanding of the passage.

An earthquake destroyed Laodicea in A.D. 61. The city was so wealthy and so self-sufficient that they rebuilt it with their own resources, refusing an offer of aid from Caesar.

## Threefold Fame

The city was famous in its day for three things. First was finance. It was a center of banking, known throughout the Roman Empire for its wealth and financial power. Second was fashion. It was renowned for the soft, black wool produced there. This wool was considered a luxury item and was sought-after for the manufacture of clothing and rugs. Laodicea was the center of fashion in its day. The newest styles appeared there first. Third were pharmaceuticals. There was a famous medical school in Laodicea, which produced a tablet that was sold all over the Roman Empire. This tablet was crushed and mixed with water to form a paste. This paste was rubbed into the eyes and was supposed to cure a variety of eye problems.

## A Laodicean Mentality

With this background in mind, consider the Lord's words of warning to this church. These words are particularly relevant in today because there are many churches like Laodicea in the world today. There are many people who call themselves Christians but who have a Laodicean mentality. Jesus came to this church without a single word of commendation. As he considered their works and their ways he had nothing good to say to them at all. He simply identified their problems. It is important not to forget why the church exists: to exalt the Savior, edify the saints and evangelize sinners, all to the ultimate glory of God. It is Christ's church. It is not a club or enclave for holy huddles. The church is not here to espouse its views but to make the Word of God known. It is not a forum to advance personal agendas or ideas. It is not a place but a people who love and honor the Lord in their lives.

Jesus died for the church. He purchased it with his own blood (Ac 20:28).[98] He builds it and he sustains it (Matt. 16:18-19; Eph. 2:19-22). The church exists for his glory. The Christian duty is to preach him; praise him; promote him; and publish him. The church belongs to God. He has bought

---

[98] Christian Publishing House would encourage the reader to consider the following article: Acts 20:28—A Worthy Translation is Faithful

http://www.christianpublishers.org/translation-acts-20-28

each individual member and so each believer is his possession.

## Lukewarm

Jesus told the Laodicean believers that like the water in their city, they have become lukewarm. As I write these words, I am in the Middle-East at the end of July during Ramadan and as anyone who lives in a hot and dry climate will attest, cool water is intensely desirable and exquisitely refreshing. In Laodicea, water from the hot springs in Hierapolis six miles away was brought into the city by aqueducts. However, by the time it reached Laodicea, the water was no longer hot; it was lukewarm. Cold water from Colossae was also piped in. However, by the time it reached Laodicea, this water was lukewarm as well. This tepid, lukewarm water meant that getting refreshment in Laodicea was difficult.

The church had also become lukewarm. This means that they had lost their passion for the things of the Lord. They had become indifferent and apathetic. They were not hostile (cold). They had reached a place where they were going through the motions, marking time and ticking boxes. They were not burning with passion for Jesus but they were not totally cold. They were somewhere in between. It seems surprising and even shocking to the average Western Christian but this kind of mediocrity makes Jesus sick. This is not overstating the case.

There is much apathy in the church in our day. The Lord wants a passionate people. Where is Christian passion for the things of the Lord? Wherever it is encountered it is a joy. There are some major problems with a church that reaches this point. This was a smug and self-satisfied church. The Lord does not complain about what they believe. They had the truth. The Lord does not complain about their practices. They were not practicing idolatry. They were complacent and the Lord detested it. The Lord is greatly displeased with lukewarm attitudes. God gave his only begotten Son to die on the cross for these people and they were indifferent. Are Christians today any better? Some churches are hot, others are cold but many, are lukewarm. The Laodicean church had a 'we heard it all before' attitude. They just don't care enough. It needs to be said again and preached in churches today throughout the world, that the Lord despises mediocrity. He is God and deserves to be honored as such.

Many people today think of Jesus as a great religious leader (such as Buddha or Mahammad).[99] They put him in that category as one who has been helpful to the human race by encouraging good morals, etc. However, they believe that he was just a man. C. S. Lewis said:

> I am trying here to prevent anyone saying the really foolish thing that people often say about Him: 'I'm ready to accept Jesus as a great moral teacher, but I don't accept His claim to be God.' That is the one thing we must not say. A man who was merely a man and said the sort of things Jesus said would not be a great moral teacher. He would either be a lunatic--on a level with the man who says he is a poached egg--or else he would be the Devil of Hell. You must make your choice. Either this man was, and is, the Son of God: or else a madman or something worse. You can shut Him for a fool, you can spit at Him and kill Him as a demon; or you can fall at His feet and call Him Lord and God. However, let us not

---

[99] I do not subscribe to the view that either of these men were great religious leaders because their teachings have led people away from the truth.

come with any patronising nonsense about His being a great human teacher. He has not left that open to us. He did not intend to.[100]

The church in Laodicea was delusional. They thought they were great. They were in denial and therefore blind to the reality of their true spiritual condition. Their perception of themselves was distorted. It is frightening to think that a proper understanding of one's spiritual condition can be so wrong. How some people see themselves and how the Lord sees them may be two different things altogether. Sadly, many churches do not understand their true spiritual condition. They do not see themselves as the Lord sees them.

## The Superlative Treasure

If a preacher was invited to speak in a church and preached a message that they (in particular) needed revival they would be offended. If he preached that the church (in general) needs revival they might listen thinking that he was speaking of others. They might agree that there are some churches somewhere that need revival but they think they are okay. The sad truth is that some are more passionate about their hobbies and recreational activities than they are about the Lord. How does a local church see itself? How does the Lord see it? What is needed more than money, more than crowds, more than fine buildings is passion for Jesus. Can the Christian honestly sing the words of the following hymn?

I'd rather have Jesus than silver or gold;
I'd rather be His than have riches untold;
I'd rather have Jesus than houses or lands;
I'd rather be led by His nail-pierced hand

---

[100] C.S. Lewis, *Mere Christianity*, Collins Fontana Religious, 1974 (23rd impression, first published 1952, pp. 55-56.

Than to be the king of a vast domain
And be held in sin's dread sway;
I'd rather have Jesus than anything
This world affords today.


I'd rather have Jesus than men's applause;
I'd rather be faithful to His dear cause;
I'd rather have Jesus than worldwide fame;
I'd rather be true to His holy name


He's fairer than lilies of rarest bloom;
He's sweeter than honey from out the comb;
He's all that my hungering spirit needs;
I'd rather have Jesus and let Him lead.[101]

Would the believer rather have him, his presence and his power more than anything material that can be named? The Christian needs him. The church needs him. The children of God must seek him and welcome him and worship him. In some ways a church is like an airplane. When an airplane stops going forward, it starts going down. When a church stops moving forward, loses its vision and stops being passionate about Jesus it is in trouble. The church in Laodicea was in trouble, but not all hope is lost. There is hope. Jesus came to give them his cure for their ailment.

Notice how Jesus came to this wayward church. Regardless of how this church saw itself, Jesus came to tell them the truth. He confronts them. He came as "the faithful and true witness". This church had a flawed understanding of itself. Jesus wanted them to know that he knew them as they

---

[101] Rhea F. Miller (1894 – 1966) ©1939 Word Music / Song Solutions CopyCare.

really were. He came to reveal their true condition and set the record straight.

### Was Jesus Created by God?

The correct meaning of the phrase "the beginning of God's creation" (v.14) is the beginner or author of God's creation. The word "beginning" is a rendering of the Greek word *archē* (ἀρχή) which means to witness, the beginning of the creation. The word refers to an originating instrument or active cause of origin (see Col. 1:15-17). William Beck translates this as "The Origin of God's creation."[102] As the creator or originator of all things, Jesus is the head and governor of all creatures; he is the king of creation (cf. Ps. 148). Jesus was not created, but was the creator of all things that were made (Col. 1:16; Heb. 1:2; 2:10). He was with the Father in the beginning, and he made all things. (Jn 1:1-3) He has always existed.

So Jesus is identified as the creator and the controller of all things. He is in control. Jesus comes to remind them that in spite of what they might think, his hand is still on the helm and he is the one with authority to guide and govern the church.

### What does Jesus Want?

Jesus is still God's final word to the church, the "Amen". He is the one who knows us best. He is the one in control, in spite of what some people may think. What is the Lord's desire for the Church? Jesus told his church that he wanted them to be either "hot or cold". He wanted the church to be a refreshing spring. He desired the church to be an oasis in

---

[102] William F. Beck, *The New Testament in the Language of Today*, Saint Louis, Missouri: Concordia Publishing House, 1963.

the desert of this world, offering healing, help and hope. He wanted his church to be a place where people can offer true heart worship and not mere lip service. Jesus said, "Well did Isaiah prophesy of you hypocrites, as it is written, "'This people honor me with their lips, but their heart is far from me'" (Mark 7:6). He wanted his church to be a place where people can have dynamic, life-changing encounters with the living God. He wanted the church to meet with him and to transact spiritual business with him. His desire has not changed for the church today.

### Conceited Christians

The Lord was displeased with this church. In fact the Lord was *disgusted* with this church. Laodicea was the last and worst of the seven churches of Asia. Jesus referred to himself as the "Amen". He is unchangeable in all his purposes and promises. Matthew Henry said, 'If religion is worth anything, it is worth everything' Christ expects his disciples to be passionate. What do Christians get passionate about?

This church is conceited. Believers should not flatter and deceive themselves. A church can become proud and carnal. The Lord does not want mere formal external observance. He wants his people to enter into the joy of loving relationship, not in a half-hearted way but in a whole-hearted manner. The church in Laodicea was in a wretched condition. It was poor but thought it was rich. It could not see its true condition but the Lord could.

The Lord clothes his children in garments of justification. He takes their rags and gives royal robes instead. Clothes are soiled with the stain of sin and need the regular cleansing of sanctification. The Lord deals with the believer's sin and shame. Matthew Henry said, 'Good counsel was given by Christ to this sinful people'. Jesus Christ told them that they could have true riches in him.

Self-confidence is a problem in the spiritual life. They were blind and needed their eyes opened. All Christians need to examine themselves in the light of Scripture. The Lord wants his people to get rid of pride, prejudices and worldly ways. The Lord rebukes because he loves.

## Misunderstood and Misused

This passage presents the picture of Jesus standing outside this church and knocking. The Lord himself is seeking to be let in. This is a verse of Scripture, which is frequently misunderstood and misused. It does not speak of Jesus outside the door of the heart of the unbeliever seeking to gain admittance. It does not teach that those who open the door of the hearts will be saved when Christ enters. This is an exegetical fallacy because these words are addressed to believers not unbelievers. Jesus was speaking to the believers in Laodicea (and, indeed, to believers today, to people in churches). He is at the door of the Christian's heart. He wants not only to *reside* in the believer by his Spirit but to *reign* in there also. Those who respond to Jesus will enjoy fellowship with him.

Jesus is speaking to believers in this text. Poor hermeneutics is at the root of this issue. Sadly, many revered heroes of history have contributed to the problem and this in turn perpetuates it among those who view the writings of such persons almost as extra-biblical literature or even sacred texts.

An example of this kind of "sanctified" misinterpretation is John Flavel's sermon "Christ knocking at the door of sinners' hearts." Flavel believed that this exhortation was directed to the visible church which consisted of saved and unsaved people.[103]

## Making Jesus Sick

The passage closes with a promise to the overcoming believer. Lukewarm attitudes are distasteful to Jesus. It makes him sick to the point of wanting to vomit. If the Christian lacks zeal for the Lord he is backslidden. The Lord says, "I will spit you out of my mouth." This implies that repentance is still possible. The Greek word used here (ἐμέω) only appears once in the New Testament. It is transliterated as *emeó* which is a verb and it means 'to vomit'. It does not mean 'to spit'. The English word 'emetic' is derived from it. An emetic is a drug often used to induce vomiting.

So properly, it means 'to vomit'. This is an example of anthropomorphism, which literally means 'man form'. It is figurative language by which God is described as having physical parts (e.g., eyes, hands, etc.), even though he is not a physical being (Jn. 4:24; Lu 24:39). In fact it also straddles what we call anthropopathism, which is a figure of speech by which human feelings or emotions are ascribed to God. This is in order to accommodate man's ignorance of the unfathomable intentions and operations of the deity (Romans 11:33-36). Alan Cole explains that anthropopathism is a figure of speech used in Exodus:

> ...by which God's activity is explained, by analogy, in strictly human terms. The meaning is not that God changed His mind; still less that He regretted something that He had intended to do. It means, in biblical language, that He now embarked

---

[103] John Flavel (c.1627–1691) the English Presbyterian clergyman, puritan, and author.

160

on a different course of action from that already suggested as a possibility, owing to some new factor which is usually mentioned in the context. In the Bible, it is clear that God's promises and warnings are always conditional on man's response: this is most clearly set out in Ezekiel 33:13-16. We are not to think of Moses as altering God's purpose towards Israel by his prayer, but as carrying it out: Moses was never more like God than in such moments, for he shared God's mind and loving purpose.[104]

Therefore, the meaning of these words of Jesus to the church in Laodicea was figurative and very potent. Jesus was saying that he was repulsed by them and desired total separation from such lukewarm attitudes. He rejected such attitudes with extreme disgust.

The message is clear: the Lord will not tolerate indifference and apathy. The word *emeo* (the verb to vomit) is not to be confused with the Greek word (ἐξέραμα) *exerama* which is the noun for vomit. This word also has only one occurrence in the New Testament where it appears in 2 Peter 2:22, "The dog returns to its own vomit." Neither is it to be confused with the Greek verb (ἐμπτύω) *emptuó*, which means 'to spit upon'. This word (and it variants, spat, spit, spitting) appears six times in the New Testament. All refer to Jesus being spat on or predicting this. The word referring to Jesus spitting to heal (blind and deaf) is different.

### Being Receptive and Responsive

The believers in Laodicea thought they had it all but Jesus told them they had nothing: "For you say, I am rich, I have prospered, and I need nothing, not realizing that you are

---

[104] Alan Cole, *Exodus*, Tyndale O.T. Commentaries, Downer's Grove, IL: InterVarsity, 1973, p. 217.

wretched, pitiable, poor, blind, and naked" (v.17). Jesus told this church exactly where they could find all they need. True riches are found in humble submission to the Lord:

## Matthew 6:19-21

¹⁹ "Do not lay up for yourselves treasures on earth, where moth and rust destroy and where thieves break in and steal, ²⁰ but lay up for yourselves treasures in heaven, where neither moth nor rust destroys and where thieves do not break in and steal. ²¹ For where your treasure is, there your heart will be also.

He can supply the garments need for impoverished people who recognize their true condition. He invited them to restore their spiritual vision. Then they would see that they needed to repent, obey and serve humbly.

A couple of years ago I realized I needed reading glasses. However, for some time before that I was in denial about it. Self-realization is hard but best. In the passage of Scripture known as The Nazareth Manifesto Jesus read these words from the scroll of Isaiah:

## Luke 4:18-19

¹⁸ "The Spirit of the Lord is upon me,
    because he has anointed me
    to proclaim good news to the poor.
He has sent me to proclaim liberty to the captives
    and recovering of sight to the blind,
    to set at liberty those who are oppressed,
¹⁹ to proclaim the year of the Lord's favor."

Christ's ministry involved offering both physical and spiritual sight to the blind. Jesus gave the Laodiceans a much-needed word of advice. In spite of their indifference toward him, he still loved them. He loved his people too much to leave them as they were. In an effort to get their attention, he rebuked them. The Lord also speaks today through his Word by the power of the Holy Spirit. Those who are receptive and responsive to the Lord will be blessed. Speaking of the Holy Spirit Jesus said, "And when he comes, he will convict the world concerning sin and righteousness and judgment" (John 16:7-11). Those who fail to heed his rebuke will be chastened. The writer to the Hebrews says, 'the Lord disciplines the one he loves, and chastises every son whom he receives' (Hebrews 12:6). He disciplines in order to deal with smug self-satisfied attitudes, if necessary.

The Lord counselled them to "be zealous and repent". He wanted them to have an energetic and unflagging enthusiasm in their walk, worship and witness. This is what he desires of every believer in every generation. Jesus closed this letter with wonderful promises: "if any man hear my voice, and open the door". This is an invitation to each individual.

## From Blessing to Backsliding

Holman Hunt's famous painting depicts Jesus standing outside a door with a lantern in his hand. He is knocking on the door. When that painting was first finished, a man looked at it and commented to the painter: "You made a mistake." Holman Hunt asked, "Where is the mistake?" The critic replied, "You forgot to paint a handle on the outside of the door." Hunt responded, "There is no mistake. The handle is on the inside. Jesus knocks, but you must open the door."

How quickly the church of the apostles moved into apostasy. The move from blessing to backsliding can happen easily and quickly. The Lord promises to those who will open the door: "I will come in to him and eat with him, and he with me" (v. 20). Here is a wonderful promise of intimacy and fellowship to those who are receptive and responsive to Jesus.

## From Backsliding to Blessing

It is possible to be a member of a lukewarm church but here is a call to each individual Christian to be what the Lord desires. If the believer opens the door to Jesus, he will come in and revive the weary life. The individual believer is responsible for his own spiritual condition and cannot blame others for his failings and shortcomings.

All the benefits of salvation will be given to the person who overcomes. They will reign with the Lord and rejoice with him in heaven. The words of the Lord to the Laodicean church challenge all Christians about their spiritual condition. Those who are saved by God's glorious grace ought to demonstrate their gratitude by being zealous and committed to the Lord and his work. The voice of Jesus still calls out to the lukewarm Christian and church today. It is important not to procrastinate on this issue, as it is both important and urgent.

Prayerfully consider the words of this beautiful song by Keith Getty and Stuart Townend:

### Speak, O Lord

Speak, O Lord, as we come to You
To receive the food of Your Holy Word.
Take Your truth, plant it deep in us;
Shape and fashion us in Your likeness,
That the light of Christ might be seen today
In our acts of love and our deeds of faith.
Speak, O Lord, and fulfill in us
All Your purposes for Your glory.

Teach us, Lord, full obedience,
Holy reverence, true humility;
Test our thoughts and our attitudes

In the radiance of Your purity.
Cause our faith to rise; cause our eyes to see
Your majestic love and authority.
Words of pow'r that can never fail—
Let their truth prevail over unbelief.

Speak, O Lord, and renew our minds;
Help us grasp the heights of Your plans for us—
Truths unchanged from the dawn of time
That will echo down through eternity.
And by grace we'll stand on Your promises,
And by faith we'll walk as You walk with us.
Speak, O Lord, till Your church is built
And the earth is filled with Your glory.[105]

# Characteristics of a Healthy Church

# Characteristics of a Healthy Church

What is a healthy church? What does God expect from all believers? What makes a church a dynamic witness in the world? Developing healthy churches is about Christians developing healthy relationships with God and with each other. Every believer has a part to play in contributing to the health of the local church by knowing the timeless truths and practical principles that contribute to the wellbeing of the local church. Each church member needs to know what his or her God-given role is and to fulfill that role. Every church should aspire to be healthy. Each Christian has a responsibility to love, serve, encourage and hold accountable each member of the church family. An essential mark of a healthy church is growth in discipleship. That means growth in holiness, love, unity and knowledge, which glorifies the Lord.

The letters of Jesus to the seven churches in Asia Minor, though insightful in terms of what Jesus approves and disapproves in church life, do not constitute a comprehensive manual on church health. They have more to say about heart-attitudes and holiness than anything else. That is because these qualities are more important than anything else is. Yet they need to be supplemented with a broader biblical perspective. In doing this great care is needed in order to avoid developing a sociological perspective that is not related to true spirituality.

## What is Church?

What is a church? According to the Bible, the church consists of the people of God. It is the community of the redeemed, the body of Christ, the bride of Christ, the fellowship of the Holy Spirit. The word 'church' does not appear in the Bible. The original Word, ἐκκλησία is a feminine noun, transliterated *ekklésia*. It refers to an assembly, or congregation. *Ekklēsía* is a compound word derived from *ek*, "*out from* and *to*" and *kaléō*, "to call"). The church, therefore, refers to people *called out from* the world and *to* God. The *English* word "church" comes from the Greek word *kyriakos*, "belonging to the Lord" (*kyrios*). *Koinonia* is the Anglicization or transliteration of the Greek word (κοινωνία). That means communion by intimate participation. It identifies the idealized state of fellowship and community that should exist within the Christian Church.

### Apolosticity

Central to a proper understanding of the church is its apostolicity. This refers to its foundation on apostolic teaching. The church is built on the foundation of the apostles and prophets (Eph.2:20), as recipients of revelation (Eph.3:4-5). There are no apostles today.[106] The word "apostle" translates from the Greek word *apostolos*. It refers to "a sent one", called, converted and commissioned with a special mission. The word is used in the New Testament to refer to those who were chosen to be the foundational leaders of the fledgling church. Thus, the apostle Paul says:

### Ephesians 2:19-22

**19** So then you are no longer strangers and aliens, but you are fellow citizens with the saints and members of the

---

[106] Some may use the term today in a different sense, especially with regard to those who are pioneer missionaries and church-planters. I am referring here to those who claim apostolic authority as recipients of revelation and composers of doctrine.

household of God, [20] built on the foundation of the apostles and prophets, Christ Jesus himself being the cornerstone, [21] in whom the whole structure, being joined together, grows into a holy temple in the Lord. [22] In him you also are being built together into a dwelling place for God by the Spirit.

They received direct revelation from God and gave it to his people. They gave the apostle's doctrine to which the early believers were devoted (Ac 2:42). There are only fourteen men in history that can wear the title of apostle. There were twelve apostles originally, until Judas defected. In Acts 1:26, Mathias was chosen to replace Judas. Paul became the fourteenth apostle (1 Cor.15:8). There are no apostles (in this sense) today.

### Nature and Purpose of the Church

People's concepts of what church is or ought to be vary widely. Some think of it in institutional terms as a college or seminary, a military academy, an army barracks, a hospital, a private club, a sort of tribal identity or cultural distinction. What does the Bible say about the nature of and purpose of church? The church is commissioned with making the unfinished task of making disciples. The Bible speaks of the church as the bride of Christ. What implications does this have? What guidelines are there in Scripture that indicate what church ought to be? What correctives are given in Scripture to churches that have deviated from what they ought to be? Addressing these questions would involve a broader study in ecclesiology and that is beyond the scope of this work. Nevertheless, an examination of what Jesus said to the seven churches in Asia Minor reveals much about what a church ought or ought not to be.

Although all but dysfunctional churches have organizational features, it ought to be borne in mind that the church is essentially an organism, that is, a living thing. This is because the Holy Spirit indwells[107] individual Christians and the Lord dwells among his assembled people.

What is the ultimate purpose of the church? What is the ideal church? How would such a church look? In what way would such a church be different from other churches in its activities? This case study in Revelation has explored these concerns.

The key characteristic of a healthy church is adherence to sound biblical theology. This is best protected and promoted by a commitment to expository preaching of the whole counsel of God. Though other forms of preaching, such as narrative and topical, can be helpful and engaging, they are not as safe as the expository model. Scripture must determine all matters of faith and practice. The Bible must guide and govern the church.

A right understanding of the gospel is critical to the life and witness of the church. Essentially that may be said to be an understanding that salvation is by grace alone, through faith alone, in Christ alone. A biblical understanding of the gospel will be clear about the necessity of conversion through repentance and faith.

Church leaders are responsible for equipping church members. This means enabling them to find ways of serving that is suited to their interests, aptitudes and gifting. This is essentially about facilitating harmonious interconnectedness.

---

[107] Christian Publishing House would encourage its readers to consider the following articles.

The Work of the Holy Spirit (esp. Biblical Interpretation) http://www.christianpublishers.org/holy-spirit-the-work-of

How Are We to Understand the Indwelling of the Holy Spirit? http://www.christianpublishers.org/holy-spirit-indwelling

A healthy church is a holy, loving, united church because God is holy, loving and united. There should not only be unity but also diversity and charity in a healthy church. A church must decide where it requires complete agreement, where it permits limited disagreement, and where it allows complete liberty. However, it must use biblical principles in so doing.

There are so many different kinds of churches, denominational, non-denominational, with differing structures in terms of government, and diverse beliefs in terms of creeds and confessions. Some churches have constitutions, which outline their core beliefs. There are broad divisions between conservative, evangelical, liberal, charismatic and cessationist churches.[108] There is a host of church models, such as house churches, mega churches and seeker-centered models as well as attractional, emerging and missional churches. Whatever the distinctive features might be, the people of God are "a chosen race, a royal priesthood, a holy nation, a people for his own possession, that [they] may proclaim the excellencies of him who called [them] out of darkness into his marvelous light."—1 Peter 2:9.

The church, as the bride of Christ, belongs to him. He cherishes her and wants to provide for her and protect her from potential harm. The church must not flirt with the world. The church is called to be faithful. The church is commissioned with the task of spreading the gospel. The

---

[108] Cessationism is the view that the "miracle gifts" of tongues and healing have ceased—that the end of the apostolic age brought about a cessation of the miracles associated with that age. Most cessationists believe that, while God can and still does perform miracles today, the Holy Spirit no longer uses individuals to perform miraculous signs. This is generally opposed to the view of continuationism (espoused by charismatic churches) which teaches that the Holy Spirit may bestow the sign gifts to persons other than the original twelve apostles, at any time in the Church age.

church is the visible manifestation of God's work on earth and it ought to glorify him.

## The Cycle of Motion and Movement

Many churches are caught in a cycle of motion without movement. They are active and busy from week to week with worship services and prayer meetings, but they are making little progress. This kind of motion is like a hamster on a wheel where the routine of activities continues in an endless cycle.

Routine is not necessarily a bad thing. In the New Testament, there is evidence of routine. Luke records that the apostle Paul gathered with the church in Troas on the first day of the week as a regular occurrence (Acts 20:7). Paul speaks of setting aside an offering on the first day of the week (1 Cor. 16:2). The writer of Hebrews urges believers not to forsake assembling together as was the habit of some (Heb. 10:23-25). Although routine may be good, it does not automatically follow that a church with a busy routine will be a healthy church. A routine in a healthy church ought to intentionally lead toward God's vision for the church: to exalt the Savior, edify the saints and evangelize sinners.

## Church Growth

Paul uses several analogies when writing about the church - agricultural (field – 1 Cor.3:6)), anatomical (body – 1 Cor. 12:12-31) and architectural (building - Eph. 2:20-22). Taking just one of these analogies, briefly, it could be said that, although the invisible church is comprised of those who are true believers, there are wheat and tares in the visible church. It is not always possible to discern one from the other, as many weeds resemble plants/crops. Growth is normally a natural sign of health. But growth must not be narrowly defined in numerical terms in a church context. Numerical growth is best understood as a potential or possible outcome of individual and corporate growth in knowledge, love and unity. In other words when a church grows towards maturity in the Word of God, love for Lord, love for the church and love for the lost it may then experience numerical growth.

Many churches that have grown large in numbers have merely added to their numbers with "transfer" growth. In other words, it is not that they have won new converts, rather, they have attracted believers as adherents of their churches. This is not, actually church growth at all.

The growth of the kingdom (church) is a sovereign act of God. The farmer prepares the soil and plants the seed. But he does not cause the growth (1 Cor. 3:6-7). The farmer is responsible for the environmental aspects of the crop. The soil must be free from weeds and rocks. There must be enough nutrients to promote healthy growth and of course water (irrigation) is a necessity. Attending to these environmental elements is the task of the farmer. Ultimately, the farmer does not make the seed grow. The seed grows independently when the conditions are right.

The topic of church growth is often reduced to issues of "more" and "bigger". However, given the reality of the visible and invisible church, size is not an adequate or accurate criterion to determine the health of a church. It is possible for a small church to be healthy and a mega-church to be unhealthy.[109] In other words, large gatherings do not necessarily constitute health when it comes to the church.

Christ made it clear that the work of building the church belongs to him (Matt. 16:18). The church is built when people are transferred from the domain of darkness to the kingdom of God. This is not something human beings can produce.

---

[109] And vice versa

There is however something that can be done. Notwithstanding the fact that church growth is the sovereign prerogative of God, one of the best ways of assisting church growth is to avoid hindering God's work. Church leaders, members and adherents have a responsibility to create and maintain an environment where the Lord's work may flourish.

### Characteristics of a Healthy Church

Much has been written in recent decades about church growth and church health. What are the biblical principles of a healthy church? A healthy church glorifies God. That must be the overall desire of every Christian individual and corporate gathering of God's people. (1 Cor.10:31). The Bible refers to the church as the body of Christ (anatomical analogy). Paul told the church in Corinth that all parts of the body are important and when one hurts the whole body hurts (1 Cor.12). This is evident in life where otherwise healthy people can experience diminished mobility simply because they have hurt their big toe. It seems small, but the impact is big. That is because there is an interdependent relationship between all the parts of the body. When one of the interconnected parts is hurt, that affects or influences the overall effectiveness of the body.

In assessing the health of any local body of believers there are a number of key areas that need a check-up.[110] These are leadership, ministry, spirituality, organization, delegation, worship, preaching and evangelism. Each of these may now be considered individually. However, they are all

---

[110] It seems that there is huge diversity of opinion regarding the selection and arrangement in order of priority of what is essential in the life of a healthy church. Every author seems to have a different set of criteria.

interconnected in terms of health, so that weakness in any area effectively weakens the overall health of the church.

## Leadership

To what extent is the ministry of the leaders focused on equipping believers for ministry.

The apostle Paul explained the purpose of leadership:

## Ephesians 4:11-13

[11] And he gave the apostles, the prophets, the evangelists, the shepherds and teachers, [12] to equip the saints for the work of ministry, for building up the body of Christ, [13] until we all attain to the unity of the faith and of the knowledge of the Son of God, to mature manhood, to the measure of the stature of the fullness of Christ,

Many of the prevailing perspectives on leadership reduce it to a set of steps, which gives the impression that leadership is a science of observable and tangible realities. However, the essence of leadership is very intangible. It is not uncommon to see a man with great leadership influence who does not fit the profile of an effective leader.

The Old Testament is filled with examples of unlikely leaders. Moses had a speech impediment. David was the youngest and was not even considered by his father as a candidate for leadership. Joseph was a dreamer and a prisoner. Daniel was a captive. Gideon was the least one in the smallest of tribes. Yet they all demonstrated great influence and effective leadership.

## Investing in Others

In the environment of a healthy church, the essential qualities or practices of leaders include a willingness to invest in others. This involves modelling the spiritual life, mentoring, and disciple making. A good leader will facilitate opportunities for those under his auspices to explore, test and develop their gifting. This is the vital function of equipping (Eph.4:11-16). It is not possible to do this effectively without delegating. There will always be an element of risk in delegation but it ought to be a calculated risk that is worth taking. One does not simply arbitrarily delegate, as this would increase the risk factor exponentially.

The idea of investment in kingdom work is illustrated by the parable of the talents from (Matt. 25). Two of the servants invested the master's money and it earned interest. But the third person was afraid. Note that the master called him "wicked" and "lazy". Instead of investing, he simply saved the money and gave it back to the master without any gain. The principle seems obvious. When a leader does not invest in the lives of others, he limits any potential increase. The investor, though taking a risk, also opens up the potential for growth. So it is with the leader who invests in others. The ministry return is increased as others are equipped and commissioned to minister. Leaders must invest in the lives of others. The role of leaders in the church is to equip the saints for the work of service for the building up of the body of Christ.

### Delegation

Equipping potential leadership does not simply mean training them, it also involves engaging them in the work of ministry (Ex. 18:17-27; 2 Tim. 4:9-22). These passages of Scripture show the need and importance of delegation. The passage in Exodus is known as "The Jethro principle". It records how Moses' father-in-law recognized the need for Moses to delegate responsibilities to others. Failure to delegate wears the leaders down and deprives potential leaders of ministry opportunities.

In 2 Timothy 4:9-22, there is a list of people to whom Paul had entrusted ministry. The apostle understood the importance of equipping and commissioning others for the ministry. It is interesting to notice several successful delegations but also a couple of failures. Such is the reality of working with flawed human beings.

Jesus practiced effective delegation. His life demonstrated a simple three-step method of delegation. Step one involved watching Jesus do it. In his early ministry, Jesus called people to follow him. This involved being with him and observing him at work (Mk. 3:13-15; Matt. 4:23; Lu 8:1). Step two involved actually doing ministry themselves. In this phase, Jesus gave instructions, watched and gave feedback (Matt. 10:1-23; Lu 10:17-20). Step three involved the disciples demonstrating to others and replicating disciples as they engaged in ministry and others observed. This is evident in the entire book of Acts—Acts 1-28.

A healthy church will consistently teach about the need for believers to be equipped for ministry. There will be a clear and accessible pathway for leadership development and new leaders will be commissioned for ministry on a regular basis. This vision needs to be consistently communicated by the leadership. If leaders in a church have distinct functions then everybody in the church ought to know exactly what their roles and responsibilities are. Leaders should be actively and intentionally mentoring and equipping others to step into significant ministry roles. The leaders' vision must be clear and others in the church must know their role in helping to accomplish that vision.

## Ministry

When it comes to ministry, the tasks in the church ought to be distributed and performed according to the spiritual gifts of individual believers. There are two distinct approaches to involving church members in ministry. The first approach views the open positions as the determining factor for the recruitment of workers. This approach considers success as "no empty positions", so the primary focus is not who fills the position, only that the position is filled. The second approach considers how God has gifted believers and then seeks to match them with an appropriate ministry that uses their spiritual gifts. This second approach is preferable.

Every believer has a unique spiritual profile. Understanding the elements of that profile will help the church become healthy in terms of the service rendered to God by the believers who make up that local body. Paul offers insight:

### 1 Corinthians 12:4-7

4 Now there are varieties of gifts, but the same Spirit; 5 and there are varieties of service, but the same Lord; 6 and there are varieties of activities, but it is the same God who empowers them all in everyone. 7 To each is given the manifestation of the Spirit for the common good.

This manifestation of the Spirit has been divided and apportioned in different ways, thus giving a multiplicity of spiritual gifts. Romans 12:6 indicates that believers have gifts that "differ according to the grace given". Everyone has the same amount of the Holy Spirit. The difference is found in the Holy Spirit's manifestation in the life of the believer. The gifts (charismaton) are a divine endowment conferred by the Holy Spirit. They are freely given by the will of God. They are not bestowed on the basis of any quality possessed by the recipient that would make them more worthy to receive the gift. A man may be a gifted communicator, intelligent, articulate and eloquent and yet not suitable to a preaching ministry. A woman may be a chartered accountant, talented with figures and more than able to keep the books and yet not a suitable candidate for appointment as an office-bearer in the role as treasurer of the church. Other factors, beside talent and training, are critical – such as humility, and teachability, to mention just two, (these qualities are interconnected) and so on.

Paul made it clear that there is one Lord of the church (the Head; Christ cf. Eph. 4:15). However, within the work of the church there are divisions of ministry. There are many different areas of ministry but service ought to bring glory to God.

Some ministries will motivate while others will not. Some want to help those who are sick, while others want to minister to women, or men, or children, or teens. God will give a burden to help direct people to a particular ministry where he wants them to serve. There are different personality traits that should be considered when a person is seeking to serve Christ in the church. Some people are temperamentally suited or unsuited to specific functions. It is essential in a healthy church that each believer understands the necessity of using their gifts for the glory of God and for the good of God's people.

The church must consistently teach that the Holy Spirit has given gifts to each believer that ought to be used in the body. A healthy church will have a working strategy for helping people discover and use their spiritual gifts. Personal spiritual giftedness must be the primary consideration before enlisting a believer to be involved in a ministry. If people are appointed to function outside their area of giftedness, they will become stressed. Every believer should be able to say confidently what his or her spiritual gift is. The ministry in which they serve should be an excellent match for their spiritual gifts. The church leadership and membership should evaluate and affirm each member's spiritual gifts regularly. People need biblical teaching on the definition and use of spiritual gifts. When ministry needs are announced in the church, the spiritual gifts needed to fulfil that ministry should also be mentioned. When this approach is taken church members will feel fruitful and fulfilled in ministry because they are serving in areas that match their giftedness.

## Spirituality

To what extent is the spiritual life of the believers in the church characterized by prayer and holiness? One cannot read the words of Jesus to the seven churches in Asia Minor without becoming convinced that a mere outward show of religion - whereby one is marking time and ticking boxes – is utterly odious to God. True spirituality is not about the mere external observance of rites and rituals. Jesus condemned the religiosity of the Pharisees because theirs was an external compliance only. They avoided murder but harbored hatred and anger, which is the source of murder. They may have avoided the physical act of adultery but by lustful thoughts, they were guilty of adultery in their hearts. They avoided making false vows but to do this they developed an elaborate system of loopholes and escapes so that they could manipulate and deceive. They prayed, fasted and gave alms to the poor but their outward acts of piety were hypocritical because they were done so as to appear holy in the eyes of others. Jesus said of them, "This people honors me with their lips, but their heart is far from me.'"—Matthew 15:7-8.

In contrast to the Pharisees, Jesus summarized the Law and the Prophets when he is spoke with a lawyer:

## Matthew 22:37-40

37 And he said to him, "You shall love the Lord your God with all your heart and with all your soul and with all your mind. 38 This is the great and first commandment. 39 And a second is like it: You shall love your neighbor as yourself. 40 On these two commandments depend all the Law and the Prophets."

In a healthy church, the leaders establish an environment where the acceptable norm of Christianity is consistent, honest prayer and discipline for the purpose of godliness and holiness. It must be remembered that the essence of true spirituality is not correct doctrine alone, but hearts that are in love with God.

Prayer is central to true spirituality. Therefore, the leaders are the ones who set the tone for the prayer culture in the church. A healthy church is an environment where the leaders exhort, and encourage people to engage in private, personal prayer with God. Jesus is the model the believer is expected to emulate. He provides an excellent example of the priority of personal (private) prayer, 'And rising very early in the morning, while it was still dark, he departed and went out to a desolate place, and there he prayed.' (Mk. 1:35). The phrase "very early in the morning" refers to the last watch of the night, which was from 3 am - 6 am. Prayer (private and corporate) is the hallmark of a healthy church. In a healthy church prayer is the first approach rather than the last resort. It is taught from the pulpit and modelled by the leaders. It is relied on and expected as a natural and vital part of the church's spiritual life.

The church must consistently teach about growing to spiritual maturity through prayer, reading the Scriptures and holy living. Personal devotions ought to be emphasized as a matter of priority. The leadership has a responsibility to model disciplined personal devotional habits. Every believer should understand the necessity of having a consistent daily time of prayer, Bible reading, meditation, worship, and Scripture memory (a practice that seems to have gone out of fashion). When this expectation is held before the people social conversations at the church will invariably turn to spiritual matters. Creating the expectation that members will engage in spiritual exercises will develop a sense of accountability. A healthy church will not only teach about biblical discipline for members who are sinning, it will also exercise discipline. The health of a church can be gauged by the attendance at the prayer meeting. Through the example of the leadership and exhortation from them, church members should be inspired to be more enthusiastic about personal holiness.

## Organization

The apostle Paul addressed both sublime theological truths and other truths that are more mundane but nonetheless necessary for the proper functioning of the church. He said, "all things should be done decently and in order."—1 Corinthians 14:40.

To what extent does the organizational structure of the church encourage and support ministry and spiritual development? The organization of a healthy church should be designed not as an end in itself but as a means to a spiritual end. It is not uncommon to see churches proliferate their organization to the point that the organization exists to perpetuate itself. An example of a runaway organizational structure can be seen in what had occurred in Judaism by the time Jesus was born.

In Exodus 20:8-11 God clearly said to remember the Sabbath day and to keep it holy. Six days humans were allowed to work but on the seventh day, they were to rest from labor according to the example given by God in the creation of the world. The Pharisees then developed an elaborate system of laws and regulations, adding over 300 stipulations to that one commandment.

In an unhealthy church, the organizational structure is cumbersome and actually hinders the free moving of the Holy Spirit. Organizational structure should be a help rather than a hindrance to the proper functioning of the church. Healthy church organization should support ministry needs:

### Acts 6:1-4

[1] Now in these days when the disciples were increasing in number, a complaint by the Hellenists arose against the Hebrews because their widows were being neglected in the daily distribution. [2] And the twelve summoned the full number of the disciples and said, "It is not right that we should give up preaching the word of God to serve tables. [3] Therefore, brothers, pick out from among you seven men of good repute, full of the Spirit and of wisdom, whom we will appoint to this duty. [4] But we will devote ourselves to prayer and to the ministry of the word."

This is an excellent example of organization that facilitates effective ministry. When the complaint arose, the apostles established a division of ministry by introducing a simple solution. They organized in such a way that the prime mission and ministry of the church would not be impeded. This was the beginning of an organizational structure that would facilitate the proclamation purposes of the church as well as the "one another" ministry of the church.[111] It was just enough organization to handle the need but not so much that it became the slave master.

This is a form of delegation similar to "The Jethro Principle" mentioned earlier (Ex. 18:17 ff.) which records how Moses' father-in-law (Jethro) gave him advice about broadening his organization with respect to judging Israel. Jethro's reasons were simple and direct: Moses would get worn out by trying to do too much and the people would lose heart because there was only one man to judge so many issues. That was inefficient and ineffective. Healthy organization will always be attached to a ministry need. Structures that are not connected to need/ministry have no real eternal purpose and instead of being a support, must be supported. When structures create needs, then people and resources go toward meeting those structural needs. This means that the structure is consuming resources that should be going toward eternally significant needs. People must always come first. Even when the structure is good, people must always come before process and programs.

Consider the example Jesus gives:

### Mark 2:23-28

[23] One Sabbath he was going through the grain fields, and as they made their way, his disciples began to pluck heads of grain. [24] And the Pharisees were saying to him, "Look, why are they doing what is not lawful on the Sabbath?" [25] And he said to them, "Have you never read what David did, when he was in need and was hungry, he and those who were with him: [26] how he entered the house of God, in the time

---

[111] There are many "one another" statements in the New Testament, such as love "one another" (Ro.12:10) and "Live in harmony with one another" (Rom.12:16) etc.

of Abiathar the high priest, and ate the bread of the Presence, which it is not lawful for any but the priests to eat, and also gave it to those who were with him?" [27] And he said to them, "The Sabbath was made for man, not man for the Sabbath. [28] So the Son of Man is lord even of the Sabbath."

The church must consistently communicate the importance of ministry and life-change over church structure. The organizational structure of the church should not be a dominant or domineering facet but it should be obvious to all members how the church is organized. Ministry must be promoted above its structure so that organizational factors are functionally designed to enhance ministry effectiveness. The organizational structure of a church should be easy to work "with" and "through" to accomplish ministry. A church is both an organism and an organization. In other words, it is a living, dynamic entity, which needs effective and efficient administration as a means of enabling it to function in accordance with its spiritual purpose. Therefore, the organizational structure of the church should serve the needs of people in the church. Sometimes the organizational structure of a church can be complex and intimidating.

### Cell-Groups

Real life ministry often takes place in smaller groups outside of the large gatherings of the church. In a healthy church, significant ministry and care takes place apart from the pastoral staff. Such whole-body ministry is contextualized in small cell groups. It is in these groups that the members of the church care for and encourage one another - under the auspices of the leadership. Each small group in the church should be a caring group that bears one another's burdens. It should be characterized by encouragement, where members of the group exhort and urge one another on to love and good deeds. There will also be accountability in the small group. Here it is less easy to hide than in a larger group. Members of the group must take holiness seriously and hold one another accountable to live for Jesus. Bible Study must have a prominent place in each small group gathering.

The church must consistently teach about the importance of each person's involvement in the small groups. Small groups will be able to minister to their members in an intensive, extensive and holistic way. It is the responsibility of the leaders in particular and all members in general to ask and encourage everybody in the church to be a part of a small group. Small groups provide opportunities for leadership development, and they are the first point of contact for the pastoral care needs of the people in the church. Small group leaders can shepherd the members of their groups proactively. Where small groups function well, those who are not a part of a small group are missing the essential ministry hub of the church. The small group ministry should be growing in visibility and significance in a healthy church.

### Worship

It is clear from reading the words of Jesus to the seven churches in Asia Minor that he desires to be the object of true heart worship. Thus worship services ought to be a God-glorifying and inspirational experience. The church needs to facilitate dynamic encounters with the living God or "God moments". Everything believers do should be to the glory of God (1 Cor.10:31). The corporate worship experience is an outpouring of individual believer's personal worship. If they have connected with God throughout the week, corporate worship is more likely to be inspirational.

Worship is not confined to the Sunday service. Worship is about how a Christian lives in humble and loving submission to the Lord. The apostle Paul said, "I appeal to you therefore, brothers, by the mercies of God, to present your bodies as a living sacrifice, holy and acceptable to God, which is your spiritual worship" (Rom.12:1). Worship involves the sacrifice of all that we are to all that we know of God. It is a lifestyle of holiness and service to God. It culminates in a sacrifice of praise to the Lord in song and service.

God desires worshipers who engage the heart, mind, and will in worship. Worshipping God in spirit and truth will be emotional, cerebral and volitional. Worship of God must be in accordance to truth. Few Christians are in danger of worshipping false gods in the crude manner of bowing down to idols and paying homage to icons. However, Christians may have idols of a different kind. These are things that take the place of God in their lives. There is also the danger of worshipping the true God in a self-styled manner. An example of this is given in the Old Testament:

### Leviticus 10:1-2

¹ Now Nadab and Abihu, the sons of Aaron, each took his censer and put fire in it and laid incense on it and offered unauthorized fire before the Lord, which he had not commanded them.² And fire came out from before the Lord and consumed them, and they died before the Lord.

Truthful, non-idolatrous, healthy, inspiring worship that receives the blessing of God must be according to his self-revelation in Scripture.

### The Regulative Principle

The Regulative principle of worship in Christian theology teaches that the public worship of God should include those and only those elements that are instituted, commanded, or appointed by command or example in the Bible. In other words, it is the belief that God institutes in Scripture whatever he requires for worship in the Church, and everything else should be avoided.

Some of the regulative principle groups reject the use of musical instruments in worship on this ground. Some might argue that adopting such a position requires the exercise of hermeneutical gymnastics in relation to some biblical texts, such as:

### Psalm 150

¹ Praise the Lord!
Praise God in his sanctuary;
   praise him in his mighty heavens!
² Praise him for his mighty deeds;
   praise him according to his excellent greatness!

   ³ Praise him with trumpet sound;
   praise him with lute and harp!
⁴ Praise him with tambourine and dance;
   praise him with strings and pipe!
⁵ Praise him with sounding cymbals;
   praise him with loud clashing cymbals!
⁶ Let everything that has breath praise the Lord!
Praise the Lord!

But those who exercise the regulative principle would contend that there is no example of musical instruments for worship in the New Testament, and/or that the Old Testament uses of instruments in worship were specifically tied to the ceremonial laws of the Temple in Jerusalem (like the Old Testament sacrificial system), and are not applicable in the church.

Many early Calvinists eschewed musical instruments in worship, and this practice typified Presbyterians, and other Reformed and Calvinist churches. In recent times, since the 1800s, most of these churches no longer exclude instruments.

The regulative principle of worship is generally practiced by the conservative Reformed churches and in other conservative Protestant denominations and it finds expression in confessional documents such as the Westminster Confession of Faith and the London Baptist Confession of Faith.

The regulative principle is often contrasted with the normative principle of worship, which teaches that whatever is not prohibited in Scripture is permitted in worship, so long as it is agreeable to the peace and unity of the Church. In other words, there must be agreement with the general practice of the Church and no prohibition in Scripture for whatever is done in worship. The normative principle of worship is the generally accepted approach to worship outside of Reformed circles as practiced widely by many denominational and independent churches.

Whatever form of worship or style of music (traditional, contemporary or blended) a church practices it must consistently teach about glorifying God through biblical worship. The words of the songs that are sung in church should be biblically accurate. It is rather strange that people who insist on this standard are deemed by many to be cranks, crackpots and nitpickers! Leaders have a duty to inspect hymns and choruses for biblical accuracy. After all the body of believers, absorb truth through the singing of psalms, hymns and spiritual songs. Worship leaders must always direct focus toward God and not the music, musicians, choir or themselves. After the worship services at church people should feel that they have been in the presence of God. The

Bible must play a significant role in the church's worship services. One should come away from a worship service feeling inspired to live for God. If God is the focus of worship it will invariably be inspiring.

### Preaching and teaching

Preaching is an act of worship. Some Christians seem to think that worship is about a section of time within the church service when hymns are sung. That is certainly worship but so too is preaching. God transforms believers by the knowledge of his Word communicated through the preaching/teaching ministry of the church. When people come with humble and open hearts and minds to hear the Word of God expounded they are engaging in worship. When people are receptive and responsive to the comfort and challenges of Scripture they are engaging in worship.

Paul describes the church as, "the household of God, which is the church of the living God, a pillar and buttress of the truth" (1 Tim.3:15). The message must not be diluted or distorted. Paul charged Timothy:

### 2 Timothy 4:1-2

¹ I charge you in the presence of God and of Christ Jesus, who is to judge the living and the dead, and by his appearing and his kingdom: ² preach the word; be ready in season and out of season; reprove, rebuke, and exhort, with complete patience and teaching.

The Word is truth (Jn. 17:17) and the whole counsel of God should be proclaimed without fear or favor.[112] To "reprove" means to correct gently and with kindly intent. This is about appealing to the mind to show a person his

---

[112] Some churches seem to be gagged by the political correctness of the age to remain silent on certain "controversial" topics.

practical and/or doctrinal error. It is to refute error and misconduct with careful biblical argument. To "rebuke" means to express sharp or stern disapproval. It is about bringing an erring person to repentance with an appeal to the heart. To "exhort" has a more positive thrust. It carries the idea of drawing alongside someone to encourage. The preaching of the word reproves the sin, rebukes the sinner and also encourages the believer to press on.

The writers of Scripture are inspired (2 Tim. 3:16-17) not individual preachers. Only when the preacher is true to the meaning of the text, will the living active Word do its work in the hearts of people. All preaching, whether narrative or topical must be biblical. Systematic expository preaching is the best diet for a healthy body of Christ.

Paul urged Timothy, "Do your best to present yourself to God as one approved, a worker who has no need to be ashamed, rightly handling the word of truth" (2 Tim. 2:15). He also said, "Until I come, devote yourself to the public reading of Scripture, to exhortation, to teaching" (2 Tim. 4:13). These duties cannot be neglected. A healthy church will consistently preach verse by verse through a book of the Bible. This will ensure that the whole counsel of God is preached. It counters the tendency to avoid certain unpalatable truths and it also counters the inclination to only preach on favorite texts.

The church's preaching ministry should mentally and spiritually transform the people of God. There is no excuse for anything less than excellent exposition of God's Word. People who attend church should learn more about the Bible each week through the church's preaching ministry. People should be motivated to study God's Word personally deeper as a result of the church's preaching ministry. The church's preaching ministry should consistently confront persons with the reality of who they are and what they should be from a biblical perspective. The church today, more than ever, needs to faithfully and consistently proclaim that the Bible is inerrant and sufficient for all life's issues. Scripture must be upheld as inspired, inerrant and authoritative in all matters of faith and practice. From week to week there ought to be biblical continuity in the preaching, where people are being taught how to understand the Bible through the preaching ministry of the church. Dull preaching is a disservice to God and his people, and it fails to communicate the glory and wonder of the gospel. After listening to the message at church, hearers should be amazed by the truth of God's Word more than they are impressed by the cleverness of the preacher or the interesting presentation.

### Evangelism

The forms of evangelistic activities must be relevant to those the church is trying to reach. Is the church giving people opportunity to respond to the gospel? Evangelism in a healthy church is a commitment to spread the message of the gospel as widely and as clearly as possible. The sovereignty of God in the process of conversion must be firmly grasped. The church must be taught to understand the role of God's sovereignty in evangelism.

God has chosen that through the message (preaching and otherwise communicated) of the gospel people would be saved, "For since, in the wisdom of God, the world did not know God through wisdom, it pleased God through the folly of what we preach to save those who believe" (1 Cor.1:21). Gospel must be proclaimed:

### Romans 10:13-14, 17

13 For "everyone who calls on the name of the Lord will be saved."

**14** How then will they call on him in whom they have not believed? And how are they to believe in him of whom they have never heard? And how are they to hear without someone preaching? **17** So faith comes from hearing, and hearing through the word of Christ.

The evangelistic efforts of a healthy church should include personal and corporate witness. If a church is to engage, effectively in evangelism there must be a heart for the lost and contact with outsiders. The church should be an extension of Christ's ministry of compassion to the world. The church must practice the ministry of compassion as an opportunity to share Christ with hungry, hurting and needy people in the community.

The church has a sacred duty to teach and preach consistently on the great commission. A healthy church will show enthusiasm for sharing the gospel as widely and as effectively as possible. Leaders should provide opportunities for people in the church to participate in regular evangelism training courses. Each local body of believers needs to seek ways to contextualize the gospel to different cultures and cultural sub-groups. Church members need to be taught to understand the essential elements of the gospel so that they feel well-equipped, confident, enthusiastic, and motivated to share their faith with others.

### The Lord has Spoken

The resurrected and ascended Lord addressed seven letters to different churches, commending them for what was worthy and condemning them for what was unworthy. Surely this record must constitute a significant statement about what Jesus expects from his church. These epistles constitute a critical canon within the canon of Scripture and as such are worthy of serious consideration by all believers and churches that desire to please the Lord. May God grant the grace needed to reflect on his words and regulate church practice in accordance with his wishes!

**Other Books by Kieran Beville**

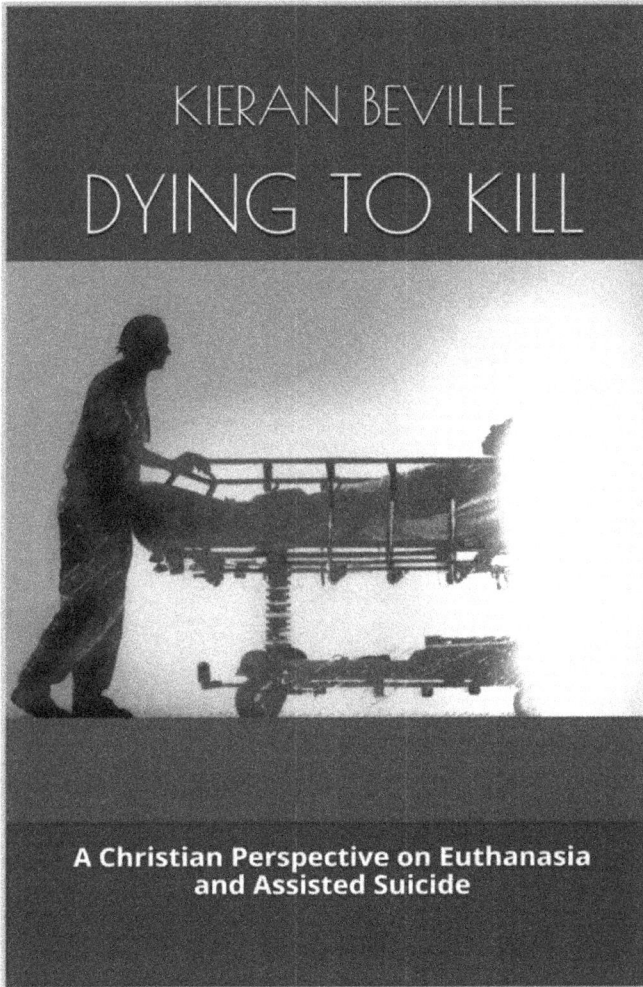

KIERAN BEVILLE
DYING TO KILL

A Christian Perspective on Euthanasia
and Assisted Suicide

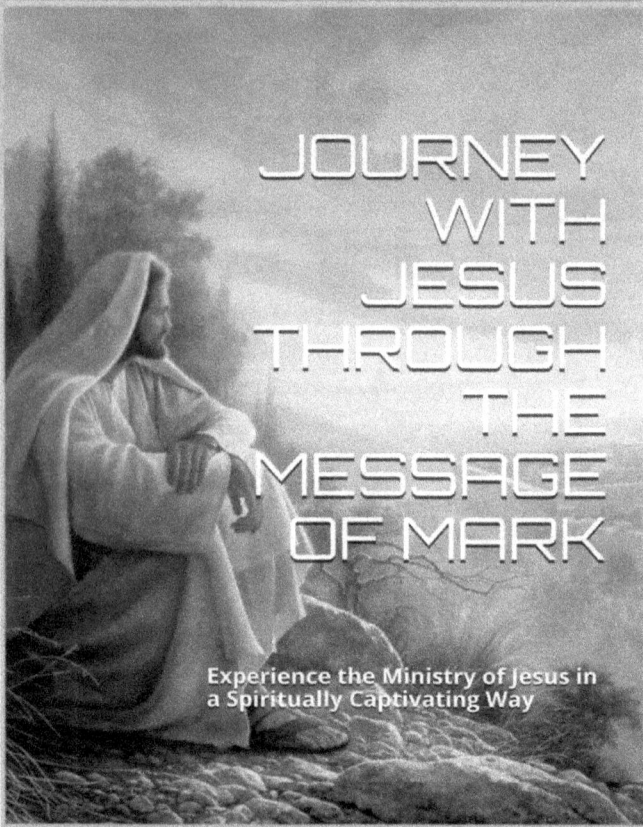

Kieran Beville

JOURNEY
WITH
JESUS
THROUGH
THE
MESSAGE
OF MARK

Experience the Ministry of Jesus in
a Spiritually Captivating Way

# Bibliography

Anderson, Leith. *"Is This Body Healthy?"* chap. in *A Church for the 21st Century.* Minneapolis, MN: Bethany House Publishers, 1992.

Andrews, Edward D. *THE EVANGELISM HANDBOOK: How All Christians Can Effectively Share God's Word in Their Community.* Cambridge: Christian Publishing House, 2013.

Andrews, Edward D. *THE CHRISTIAN APOLOGIST: Always Being Prepared to Make a Defense .* Cambridge: Christian Publishing House, 2014.

—. *THE CHRISTIAN EVANGELIST Go Therefore and Make Disciples In Your Own Community! (VOLUME 1).* Cambridge: Christian Publishing House, 2013.

Arnold, Clinton E. *Zondervan Illustrated Bible Backgrounds Commentary Volume 4: Hebrews to Revelation.* Grand Rapids, MI: Zondervan, 2002.

Beck, William F. *The New Testament in the Language of Today.* Saint Louis: Concordia Publishing House, 1963.

Berkhof, Louis. *Principles of Biblical Interpretation.* Grand Rapids, MI: Baker Book House, 1994.

Bowen, Murray. *Family Therapy in Clinical Practice.* Northvale, NJ: Jason Aronson, 1994.

Brand, Chad, Charles Draper, and England Archie. *Holman Illustrated Bible Dictionary: Revised, Updated and Expanded.* Nashville, TN: Holman, 2003.

Campbell, Barry. *Smaller Churches Healthy and Growing.* Nashville, TN: LifeWay Press, 1998.

Corey, Gerald. *Theory and Practice of Counseling and Psychotherapy, 6th ed.* Belmont, CA: Wadsworth, 2001.

Dever, Mark. *Nine Marks of a Healthy Church.* Wheaton, IL: Crossway Books, 2000.

Easley, Kendell H. *Holman New Testament Commentary, vol. 12, Revelation.* (Nashville, TN: Broadman & Holman Publishers, 1998.

Eckman, James P. *Exploring Church History* . Wheaton, Ill: Crossway, 2002.

Ellas, John, and Flavil Yeakley. "Review of Natural Church Development, by Christian A. Schwarz." *Journal of the American Society for Church Growth*, Spring 1999: 83-92.

Falwell, Jonathan. *Innovate Church.* Nashville, TN: B&H Publishing Group, 2008.

Ferguson, Everett. *CHURCH HISTORY VOLUME ONE: From Christ to Pre-Reformation.* Grand Rapids: Zondervan, 2005.

Furnish, Victor Paul. *The Love Commandment in the New Testament.* Nashville, TN: Abingdon Press, 1972.

Geisler, Norman, and David Geisler. *CONVERSATION EVANGELISM: How to Listen and Speak So You Can Be Heard.* Eugene: Harvest House Publishers, 2009.

Geisler, Norman, and Ron Rhodes. *Conviction Without Compromise.* Eugene, OR.: Harvest House Publishers, 2008.

Getz, Gene. *The Measure of a Church.* Glendale, CA: Regal Books, 1973.

Gregg, Steven. *Four Views of Revelation*. Nashville: Thomas Nelson Publishers, 1997.

Guralnik, David B. *Webster's New World Dictionary, 2d college ed*. New York, NY: Simon and Schuster, 1984.

Hanegraaff, Hank. *The Apocalypse Code*. Nashville: Thomas Nelson, 2007.

Hemphill, Ken. *The Antioch Effect: 8 Characteristics of Highly Effective Churches*. Nashville, TN: Broadman & Holman Publishers, 1994.

Hesselgrave, David J. *Planting Churches Cross-Culturally*. Grand Rapids: Baker Academic, 2000.

Hewitt, Gerald Neal. *A Prescription for Healthy Churches: Help for Disintegrating Churches and Directionless Pastors*. Winston-Salem, NC: GNH Publishing, 2001.

Hodge, Dean R., David A. Roozen, and eds. *Understanding Church Growth and Decline: 1950-1978*. New York: The Pilgrim Press, 1979.

Kaiser, Walter C, and Moises Silva. *Introduction to Biblical Hermeneutics: The Search for Meaning*. Grand Rapids: Zondervan, 1994, 2007.

LaHaye, Tim, Thomas Ice, and ed. *The End Times Controversy*. Eugene, OR: Harvest House Publishers, 2003.

Lange, J. P. *Commentary of the Holy Scriptures: Revelation*. New York: Scribner's, 1872.

LaSor, William. *'Interpretation of Prophecy', Hermeneutics, ed. Bernard Ramm*. Grand Rapids, MI: Baker, 1987.

Logan, Robert E. *Beyond Church Growth: Action Plans for Developing a Dynamic Church*. Grand Rapids, MI: Fleming H. Revell, 1989.

Macchia, Stephen A. *Becoming a Healthy Church: 10 Characteristics.* Grand Rapids, MI: Baker Books, 1999.

Macchia, Stephen. *Becoming a Healthy Church Workbook: A Dialogue, Assessment, and Planning Tool.* Grand Rapids, MI: Baker Books, 2001.

Masters, Peter. *Do We Have a Policy for Church Health & Growth: Paul's Ten Point Policy.* London: The Wakeman Trust, 2002.

McCarthy, Dan, and Charles Clayton. *Let the Reader Understand: A guide to Interpreting and Applying the Bible.* Wheaton, Illinois: BridgePoint, 1994.

McGavran, Donald A., and Win Arn. *How to Grow a Church: Conversations about Church Growth.* Glendale, CA: Regal Books, 1973.

McReynolds, Paul R. *Word Study: Greek-English.* Carol Stream: Tyndale House Publishers, 1999.

Milligan, William. *The Book of Revelation.* London: Hodder and Stoughton, 1889.

Mitchell, Michael R. *Leading, Teaching, and Making Disciples: World-Class Education in the Church, School, and Home.* Bloomington: Crossbooks, 2010.

Morris, Leon. *Tyndale New Testament Commentaries: Revelation.* Grand Rapids: William Eerdmans Publishing Company, 1987.

Mounce, Robert. *Robert Mounce, The New International Commentary of the New Testament: The Book of Revelation.* Grand Rapids: William Eerdmans Publishing Company, 1977.

Mounce, William D. *Mounce's Complete Expository Dictionary of Old & New Testament Words*. Grand Rapids, MI: Zondervan, 2006.

Osborne, Grant R. *BAKER EXEGETICAL COMMENTARY ON THE NEW TESTAMET: REVELATION*. Grand Rapids, MI: Baker Academic, 2002.

Reid, Alvin L. *Radically Unchurched: Who They are and How to Reach Them*. Grand Rapids: Kregel, 2002.

Richardson, Ronald. *Creating a Healthier Church: Family Systems Theory, Leadership, and Congregational Life*. Minneapolis, MN: Fortress Press, 1996.

Robertson, Paul E. "Theology of the Healthy Church." *The Theological Educator: A Journal of Theology and Ministry*, Spring 1998: 45-52.

Robinson, Darrell W. *Total Church Life: How to be a First Century Chrurch*. Nashville, TN: Briadman and Holman, 1997.

Ryrie, Charles. *Dispensationalism*. Chicago: Moody Publishers, 2007.

Spader, Dan, and Gary Mayes. *Growing a Healthy Church*. Chicago: Moody Press, 1991.

Sproul, R.C. *Knowing Scripture.* . Downers Grove, IL: Intervarsity Press, 1978.

Stedman, Ray C. *"Keeping the Body Healthy,"* In *Body Life: The Church Comes Alive!* Ventura, CA: Regal Books, 1972.

Steinke, Peter L. *Healthy Congregations*. Bethesda, MD: Alban Institute, 1996.

—. *How Your Church Family Works*. Bethesda, MD: Alban Institute, 1993.

Stuart, Moses. *A Commentary on the Apocalypse*. Edinburgh: Maclachlan: Stewart & Co., 1847.

Tenney, Merrill. *Interpreting Revelation*. Grand Rapids: William Eerdmans Publishing Company, 1957.

Thomas, Robert L. *Revelation 1-7: An Exegetical Commentary*. Chicago, IL: Moody Publishers, 1992.

—. *Revelation 8-22: An Exegetical Commentary*. Chicago, IL: Moody Publishers, 1995.

Tidwell, Charles A. *Church Administration: Effective Leadership for Ministry*. Nashville, TN: Broadman & Holman Publishers, 1985.

Wagner, C. Peter. *Your Church Can Grow: Seven Vital Signs of a Healthy Church*. Glendale, CA: Regal Books, 1976.

Walvoord, John. *The Revelation of Jesus Christ*. Chicago: Moody Press, 1996.

Warren, Rick. *The Purpose Driven Church: Growth without Compromising Your Message & Mission*. Grand Rapids, MI: Zondervan Publishing House, 1995.